BEYOND THE MOLECULE

THE ART AND SCIENCE OF METAPHORS THAT MATTER

BEYOND THE MOLECULE

THE ART AND SCIENCE OF METAPHORS THAT MATTER

Subba Rao Chaganti

PharmaMed Press
An imprint of BSP Books Pvt. Ltd.
4-4-309/316, Giriraj Lane,
Sultan Bazar, Hyderabad - 500 001.

Beyond the Molecule: The Art and Science of Metaphors That Matter
by Subbarao Chaganti

Published by

™ **PharmaMed Press**
An imprint of BSP Books Pvt. Ltd.
4-4-309/316, Giriraj Lane, Sultan Bazar, Hyderabad - 500 001.
Phone: 040-23445688
E-mail: info@pharmamedpress.net
www.bspbooks.net/www.pharmamedpress.net

ISBN: 978-93-47311-55-0 (Hardbound)

Disclaimer

The information, ideas, and guidance presented in this book **"Beyond the Molecule: The Art and Science of Metaphors That Matter"** are provided for educational and informational purposes only. This book is intended for professionals working in pharmaceutical marketing, healthcare communication, and related fields.

The metaphors, examples, and case studies presented in this book should be viewed as illustrative rather than prescriptive. While every effort has been made to ensure the accuracy and effectiveness of the approaches discussed, the author and publisher make no warranties or representations regarding the outcomes that may result from implementing these strategies.

Readers should note that all case studies have been anonymized. While they reflect actual marketing campaigns and their outcomes, specific details may have been altered to protect proprietary information and company identities. Any resemblance to specific products or campaigns beyond those explicitly named is coincidental.

The regulatory environment for pharmaceutical marketing varies substantially by country and jurisdiction. The approaches described in this book should always be adapted to comply with local regulations and legal requirements. Readers are responsible for ensuring that any metaphors or communication strategies they implement comply with relevant advertising standards, regulatory guidelines, and ethical principles governing healthcare communication in their respective regions.

This book is not a substitute for legal, regulatory, or medical advice. Before implementing marketing strategies for pharmaceutical products, readers should consult with appropriate legal, regulatory, and medical experts.

The metaphors presented in this book should never be used to misrepresent or exaggerate the effects, benefits, or mechanisms of action of any medication or treatment. The ethical principles outlined in Chapter 9 are essential considerations in all applications of the concepts presented herein.

Neither the author nor the publisher shall be liable for any loss or damage allegedly arising from any information or suggestion in this book.

Preface

In the nearly six decades I've spent in pharmaceutical marketing, I've noticed an interesting trend. The most scientifically advanced treatments—breakthrough therapies that represent genuine innovation—often struggle the most to gain understanding and acceptance. Meanwhile, simpler products with more accessible concepts frequently achieve faster adoption, even when their clinical benefits are more modest.

This paradox led me to the central question that inspired this book: Why do some complex scientific concepts connect immediately with healthcare stakeholders, while others—despite their significance—remain frustratingly hard to comprehend?

The answer, I found, often boils down to metaphor.

When I first started exploring this territory, I expected to find metaphors mainly as creative flourishes—helpful linguistic tools that make technical information more engaging. What I discovered instead was something much more fundamental. The right metaphor doesn't just embellish information; it transforms how people understand, remember, and act on it.

In the pages that follow, you will find that metaphors operate at the intersection of cognitive science, linguistics, and behavioral psychology. They provide essential frameworks that help our brains process complex information. In healthcare specifically, they act as bridges between the microscopic world of molecular activity and the human experience of health and illness.

This book is the result of both research and real-world application. It draws on cognitive studies that demonstrate how metaphors shape our thinking, interviews with patients about what helped them understand their conditions, conversations with physicians on how they explain complex treatments, and collaborations with pharmaceutical marketing teams aimed at communicating breakthrough therapies.

Whether you are a marketer explaining a novel mechanism of action, a medical affairs specialist preparing educational materials, or a communications professional crafting messages about value and outcomes, I hope this book transforms how you approach your work. The frameworks, case studies, and practical tools provided here are not merely theoretical—they are designed for immediate application to your specific challenges.

Throughout these pages, you'll find that effective metaphors are not just creative exercises. They are strategic tools that require careful development, testing, and refinement. When executed well, they not only make science more accessible, but they also make it more meaningful, memorable, and actionable.

In a healthcare landscape of increasing complexity—from personalized medicine to digital health integration—the ability to foster understanding through effective metaphors has never been more valuable. This skill can determine whether a breakthrough therapy shifts the standard of care or fails to reach the patients who need it.

My sincere hope is that this book helps you bridge the gap between complex science and human understanding in ways that ultimately benefit patients. In healthcare, effective communication isn't just good marketing; it's good medicine.

Subba Rao Chaganti
Farmington, Connecticut
March 2025

Acknowledgements

This book would not have been possible without the support, guidance, and expertise of many individuals who contributed in ways both large and small.

First, I extend my deepest gratitude to Anil Shah, whose vision as a publisher and unwavering belief in this project helped transform a concept into the book you hold today. His editorial insights and commitment to excellence shaped this work in countless ways. I am also indebted to Nikunjesh Shah for his pioneering work in making the digital editions available and ensuring that this content reaches readers across multiple platforms.

The visual appeal and user-friendly design of this book are thanks entirely to Naresh Daver and his talented team at PharmaMed Press.

I am grateful to the many pharmaceutical marketing professionals who generously shared their experiences, challenges, and successes with me during my research. Special thanks to the healthcare providers, patients, and advocates who provided perspectives that kept this work grounded in the real-world impact of effective communication.

My colleagues at various research institutions and pharmaceutical companies deserve special mention for their willingness to review drafts, provide case studies, and challenge my thinking. Their collective wisdom runs throughout these pages.

On a more personal note, I owe everything to my family, whose patience and encouragement sustained me throughout this journey. To my spouse, Mahalakshmi, whose unwavering support created the space for me to pursue this project, your partnership makes everything possible. To my children and their spouses—Srinivasa Phanindra, Geetha, Lavanya, Satya Sankara Aditya, Sowmya, and Chaitanya—thank you for your constant encouragement and understanding during the many family gatherings where my mind occasionally wandered to metaphor frameworks.

And to my grandchildren—Aditi, Eesha, Surya, and Shriya—your curiosity and natural ability to explain complex things through simple comparisons frequently reminded me why this work matters. You are the ultimate metaphor creators, and your fresh perspectives often illuminated new approaches I hadn't considered.

Finally, I want to extend my appreciation to you, the reader, for recognizing the importance of effective communication in healthcare. I hope that the frameworks and insights in these pages help you create understanding that ultimately benefits patients, because in the end, that's what this work is truly about.

Subba Rao Chaganti

Farmington, Connecticut

July 2025

Contents

PART II: STRATEGIC APPLICATIONS IN PHARMA

PART III: IMPLEMENTATION AND BEST PRACTICES

CHAPTER 8

CHAPTER 9

PART IV: CASE STUDIES AND EXAMPLES

CHAPTER 10

CHAPTER 11

PART I: FOUNDATIONS OF METAPHOR IN COMMUNICATION

Part I

Foundations of Metaphors in Communication

In the simplest terms, metaphors are ways of describing something by comparing it to something else that people already understand. They're powerful tools that help us grasp complex ideas, rather than relying solely on flowery language or creative writing tricks.

What Metaphors Are

A metaphor is when you talk about one thing in terms of another. When a doctor says, "Your immune system is like an army fighting invaders," they're not being poetic; they're helping you understand how your body works by comparing it to something familiar (an army).

Why Our Brains Love Metaphors

Our brains naturally think in comparisons and associations. When we encounter something new or complex (like how a medication works), we try to connect it to concepts we already know. This is why a good metaphor feels like an "aha!" moment - it creates a bridge between the unknown and the known.

When you hear "this drug acts as a key that unlocks specific receptors," you immediately grasp the mechanism without needing to understand detailed biochemistry.

Types of Metaphors That Work

1. **Conceptual metaphors** shape our understanding of entire domains. In healthcare, we often use journey metaphors ("the path to recovery") or battle metaphors ("fighting disease").
2. **Visual metaphors** represent ideas through images. Showing a medication as a shield protecting a cell makes its function instantly understandable.

3. **Narrative metaphors** tell a story that parallels the real process. Describing T-cells as "trained security guards that learn to recognize threats" provides people with a clear storyline to follow.

The Science Behind Why Metaphors Work

When we process metaphors, multiple areas of our brain activate simultaneously—the language centers and the sensory regions associated with the comparison. This deeper processing leads to:

- Better retention of information
- Stronger emotional connections to the message
- More intuitive understanding of complex concepts
- Easier recall when making decisions

This is why pharmaceutical messages that use appropriate metaphors tend to be more memorable and persuasive than those filled with technical jargon alone.

Chapter One

Introduction: The Power of Metaphor in Healthcare Communication

Imagine trying to explain to someone how a complex medication works in their body without using any comparisons. You could end up with technical terms that leave them confused and disconnected. This is the everyday challenge in pharmaceutical marketing.

Why Healthcare Communication Is Uniquely Challenging

Healthcare and medicine involve complex science that most people don't encounter in their daily lives. When marketing pharmaceutical products, you're often trying to:

- Explain invisible processes happening at a molecular level
- Communicate statistical benefits and risks meaningfully
- Bridge the knowledge gaps between experts and non-experts
- Connect emotionally with people about sensitive health issues

Regular marketing language often falls short here.

How Metaphors Transform Healthcare Messages

Metaphors cut through this complexity by using familiar concepts to explain unfamiliar ones. When a medication that prevents blood clots is described as a "traffic officer keeping blood flowing smoothly," people immediately grasp its function.

Good metaphors in healthcare:

- Turn abstract concepts into concrete images
- Simplify without being misleading
- Create emotional connections to clinical information

- Help people remember key information when making decisions
- Bridge communication gaps between different stakeholders

Real Impact on Stakeholders

For patients, metaphors can transform fear of the unknown into understanding. "Cancer treatment shrinks tumors like water shrinks a sponge," gives patients a mental image they can hold onto.

For doctors, metaphors provide shortcuts to explain complex treatments to patients in a limited time. "This medication works like a dimmer switch for your immune system" quickly conveys how a biologic might work.

For payers and decision-makers, metaphors help illustrate value beyond numbers. Describing preventative medicine as an "insurance policy against costlier interventions" frames the economic argument in familiar terms.

The right metaphor doesn't just make pharmaceutical marketing more creative—it makes it more effective, ensuring that vital health information not only reaches people but also resonates with them in a way that influences their decisions and behaviors.

The Unique Communication Challenges in Pharmaceutical Marketing

Pharmaceutical marketing encounters some unique challenges that most other product marketing does not face.

Rules Everywhere

Unlike selling shoes or soft drinks, every word in pharmaceutical marketing is heavily regulated. You can't make claims without solid proof; you must include side effects alongside benefits, and certain phrases might be completely off-limits. It's like trying to write a creative story while following a very strict rulebook.

Really Complicated Products

Medicines rely on complex science that most people don't understand. Try explaining how a monoclonal antibody targets specific proteins without confusing your audience! Finding simple ways to describe these complicated products without being misleading is very challenging.

Talking to Different Groups at Once

Pharmaceutical marketers often need to reach:

- Doctors who understand medical terminology
- Patients who want to know how it helps them
- Insurance companies that care about cost-effectiveness
- Regulators who scrutinize every claim

Each group needs different information presented in different ways.

Serious Consequences

If someone misunderstands an ad for potato chips, not much happens. If someone misunderstands information about a medication, it can impact important health decisions. This creates a special responsibility to be clear and accurate.

Emotional Topics

Health conditions often trigger fear, worry, or embarrassment. Marketing needs to be considerate of these feelings while still conveying messages clearly. Some common marketing strategies might come across as inappropriate or insensitive when addressing serious illnesses.

Invisible Benefits

Many medicines work in ways patients can't see or feel directly. How do you demonstrate the value of something that's silently preventing a problem? This requires creative approaches to make invisible benefits feel real and significant.

Building Trust Over Time

Pharmaceutical marketing aims to foster long-term treatment and trust. The messages must not only capture attention but also foster understanding that encourages people to stay committed to their treatment over months or years.

These unique challenges make good metaphors highly valuable in pharmaceutical marketing—they transform complex science into clear concepts that resonate with diverse audiences while following regulations and respecting the serious nature of healthcare choices.

Why Metaphors Matter in Complex Scientific Communication

Metaphors are essential for explaining complex scientific concepts because they serve as bridges between unfamiliar ideas and what people already understand.

Making the Invisible Visible

Many scientific processes happen at levels we can't see - inside cells, at the molecular level, or through chemical reactions. Metaphors give these invisible processes a visible form. When we describe antibodies as "security guards recognizing intruders," suddenly an abstract immune process becomes something people can visualize.

Simplifying Without Dumbing Down

Good metaphors don't oversimplify science - they provide a framework for understanding it. Comparing the targeted action of a cancer drug to a "smart missile that only hits specific targets" helps people grasp the concept of precision without requiring a degree in oncology.

Creating Emotional Connection

Pure scientific facts rarely evoke emotions, but health decisions are often emotionally charged. Metaphors help build this emotional bridge. Describing cholesterol buildup as "rust in your pipes" creates both understanding and motivation to address the problem.

Improving Memory and Recall

People tend to remember stories and images more effectively than technical facts. A patient might forget the term "anticoagulant," but they'll remember their doctor describing their blood thinner as a "traffic officer keeping blood flowing smoothly." This improved recall facilitates treatment adherence and informed health decisions.

Bridging Knowledge Gaps

The gap between expert knowledge and public understanding can be enormous in healthcare. Metaphors help cross this divide. When a doctor compares diabetes management to "balancing a seesaw," it provides patients with a mental model they can use to better understand their condition.

Building Shared Understanding

Different stakeholders (patients, doctors, family members) need to communicate about complex conditions. Metaphors create a shared language. When everyone understands the "lock and key" metaphor for how medication works, conversations become more productive.

In essence, metaphors matter because they turn complex scientific information from something intimidating and foreign into something familiar and manageable, which is crucial for making informed healthcare decisions.

Overview of the Book's Approach

This book offers a practical, step-by-step guide to using metaphors effectively in pharmaceutical marketing. Here's what you'll learn:

Starting with the Basics

We start by explaining what metaphors really are and why they are so effective at clarifying complex medical ideas. We simplify the science behind how our brains understand metaphors.

Moving to Real-World Applications

Rather than just theory, we focus on how to create and use metaphors in your pharmaceutical marketing. You'll learn specific approaches for:

- Different audiences (doctors, patients, insurance companies)
- Various health conditions (chronic diseases, cancer, rare disorders)
- Different marketing channels (digital, print, presentations)

Learning from Success Stories

We provide clear examples of powerful metaphors in pharmaceutical marketing. We examine case studies that simplify complex treatments and build emotional bonds with people.

Practical Tools You Can Use Right Away

The book includes worksheets, checklists, and frameworks that you can use for your marketing challenges. We provide a step-by-step process to develop effective metaphors tailored to your unique situation.

Looking to the Future

Finally, we explore how digital technology is changing the use of metaphors in healthcare and highlight emerging trends you should watch for.

This book uses clear language and includes numerous examples, helping you to apply these concepts right away. Our goal is to give you practical skills to boost your pharmaceutical marketing effectiveness through well-crafted metaphors.

Chapter Two

Understanding Metaphors: Theoretical Frameworks

What Metaphors Are

At their core, metaphors are ways of understanding one thing through another. When we say "your immune system is your body's defense force," we're not just being colorful – we're using something familiar (a defense force) to explain something complex (the immune system).

Metaphors are more than just decorative language. They are essential tools our minds use to understand complex ideas.

How Metaphors Shape Our Thinking

Cognitive scientists have found that metaphors shape our thoughts. When we use the metaphor "time is money" (we "spend" time, "save" time, "waste" time), it influences how we perceive and value time in our culture.

In healthcare, metaphors like "fighting disease" or "the patient journey" not only describe experiences but also influence how people view their health conditions and the treatments connected to them.

Different Types of Metaphors That Work in Healthcare

1. **Conceptual metaphors** are broad comparisons that influence whole ideas. For example, the concept "the body is a machine" leads to describing the heart as a "pump" and arteries as "pipes."
2. **Visual metaphors** use images to communicate ideas. Showing a medication as a key that fits into a lock makes its mechanism instantly clear, without using technical jargon.
3. **Narrative metaphors** tell a story that mirrors the real process. Describing how a vaccine "trains" the immune system to recognize threats gives people a storyline they can follow.

The power of metaphors in healthcare communication is that they aren't just decorative—they serve a purpose. They help connect complex medical science with everyday understanding, so different stakeholders can truly understand what matters about pharmaceutical products.

Defining Metaphor: Beyond Literary Device

Most of us first learned about metaphors in English class as figures of speech used in poetry or literature. However, metaphors are much more than just tools for creative writing.

More Than Just Fancy Language

A metaphor isn't just a decorative way of expressing something. When a doctor says that certain cells act as "sentinels" in your immune system, it's not just colorful language – it's a strong way to help you understand how these cells work.

How We Think

Cognitive scientists have found that metaphors show how our brains work naturally. Our minds constantly connect different ideas and experiences to understand new concepts. We think in terms of comparisons and associations all the time, even when we're not aware of it.

Metaphors as Mental Tools

Metaphors act as mental tools that assist us:

- **Grasp abstract concepts** by connecting them to concrete experiences
- **Simplify complexity** without losing important meaning
- **Process new information** by linking it to what we already know
- **Remember key points** by attaching them to memorable images

In Everyday Thinking

We use metaphors constantly in daily thinking:

- When we talk about "building" an argument
- When we describe depression as feeling "down"
- When we speak of "fighting off" a cold
- When we talk about "navigating" healthcare systems

These aren't just expressions – they reflect how we understand these concepts.

In Healthcare Specifically

In healthcare, metaphors act as crucial links between scientific facts and human experience. When we describe a selective medication as a "key that fits only one lock," we create a mental image that helps people grasp how the drug works without needing advanced biochemical knowledge.

What makes metaphors so powerful in pharmaceutical marketing isn't their literary beauty; it's their ability to turn complex medical ideas into something familiar and clear for different audiences.

Cognitive Metaphor Theory: How Metaphors Structure Thinking

The Big Idea in Simple Terms

Cognitive metaphor theory argues that metaphors are more than decorative language - they are essential ways our brains understand complex ideas. Instead of just poetic expressions, metaphors serve as fundamental tools for our minds to interpret the world.

How It Works in Real Life

Think about how we talk about arguments. We use phrases like:

- "I attacked his weak points."
- "She defended her position."
- "His claims are indefensible."
- "She shot down all my arguments."

This reveals something important: we don't just TALK about arguments as if they were battles - we actually THINK about them that way. The "argument is war" metaphor influences how we handle disagreements.

Why This Matters in Healthcare

In healthcare, the metaphors we use greatly influence how people perceive their conditions and treatments.

- If we use "body is a machine" metaphors, people think about "fixing" parts and "maintaining" systems.
- If we use "illness is a journey" metaphors, people focus on progress, setbacks, and moving forward.
- If we use "medicine is a shield" metaphors, people think about protection and defense
- These aren't just different ways of saying the same thing; they create distinct understandings in people's minds.

How We Build Understanding Through Metaphors

Our brains constantly connect what we already know to what we don't know. When trying to understand how a new medication functions, we instinctively search for familiar ideas to help us comprehend it.

If someone describes an antibiotic as a "bacteria killer," you immediately understand what it does. But if they say it "disables the bacteria's ability to build cell walls," you might have trouble understanding without a biology background.

The Power This Gives Communicators

When you realize that metaphors shape how we think, you become a more powerful communicator. By choosing metaphors carefully, you can help people understand complex medical ideas in ways that feel natural and clear to them.

The right metaphor doesn't just describe; it fosters understanding by linking new information to existing mental frameworks, making the unfamiliar seem familiar.

Types of Metaphors: Conceptual, Visual, and Narrative

Conceptual Metaphors

These are the broad frameworks that influence how we view entire topics. They're often so ingrained in our thinking that we're unaware of them.

Example: The phrase "The body is a machine" is a conceptual metaphor that encourages us to think of the heart as a "pump," arteries as "pipes," and maintenance as "tune-ups" (or check-ups).

In pharma marketing, describing the immune system as a "defense system" influences how people understand all aspects of immunity - from "invading" viruses to "first-line defenses" and "targeted responses."

Visual Metaphors

These use images or visual comparisons to explain ideas. They help people literally "see" the concept in their mind's eye.

Example: Comparing a medication to a key that fits precisely into a specific lock to illustrate targeted therapy.

Visual metaphors are particularly effective in patient education materials and presentations. A simple image depicting cholesterol as "gunk clogging pipes" conveys the message more effectively than paragraphs of text about arterial plaque.

Narrative Metaphors

These tell a story or describe a sequence of events that parallels the actual process. They give people a storyline to follow.

Example: Explaining how a vaccine "trains" the immune system by introducing a harmless version of a threat, so it can "recognize" and "remember" the real threat later.

Narrative metaphors are effective for illustrating treatments over time. Describing cancer treatment as a "marathon, not a sprint" helps establish realistic expectations for the journey ahead.

Each type of metaphor addresses different communication needs in pharmaceutical marketing. The most effective communication often combines various types—using a conceptual framework supported by visual elements and wrapped in a narrative that helps stakeholders grasp the full picture.

Chapter Three

The Neuroscience of Metaphor: Why Our Brains Respond

How Our Brains Process Metaphors

When you hear a metaphor like "this drug is a key that unlocks your cells," something fascinating occurs in your brain. Instead of simply processing words, your brain activates multiple regions:

- The language areas light up to process the words
- The visual areas that would activate if you were looking at keys and locks
- The motor areas that would be involved in the physical action of unlocking
- This creates a richer, more complete understanding than literal language alone.

Why This Creates Stronger Connections

This multi-region brain activation does several important things:

1. **Deeper Processing**: When you engage more of your brain, metaphors form stronger neural connections and improve memory formation.
2. **Emotional Engagement**: Metaphors frequently connect to sensory experiences that evoke emotions, thus enhancing the emotional impact of factual information.
3. **Concrete Understanding**: Abstract ideas are connected to physical experiences we've had in the real world, making them seem more tangible.

The Memory Advantage

Studies show that information presented through metaphors is generally remembered better than the same information presented literally. When a doctor describes a medication as a "shield protecting your cells," patients are more likely to remember its protective role than if the doctor calls it a "preventative agent."

The Decision-Making Connection

Our brains decide partly based on emotions and partly on understanding. Metaphors impact both:

- They enhance comprehension of complex information
- They create emotional resonance with otherwise clinical information

This combination helps people make more confident healthcare decisions because they both understand and connect with the information.

Why Some Metaphors Work Better Than Others

The most effective metaphors in healthcare connect with shared experiences and emotions. For instance, comparing blood vessels to highways works well because most people understand traffic flow. Conversely, comparing a medication to a complex computer algorithm may not be as effective since many people lack a clear reference point.

This is why it is essential to understand your audience when crafting effective metaphors in pharmaceutical marketing.

Neural Processing of Figurative Language

How Your Brain Handles Metaphors

When you hear straightforward literal language like "this medication reduces inflammation," your brain primarily processes it in the language regions on the left side.

But when you hear a metaphor like "this medication is a fire extinguisher for inflammation," something different occurs.

1. Your brain first processes the basic language in the usual language areas
2. Then it activates areas that handle visual imagery and sensory experiences
3. It also activates motor areas that would be involved if you were using a fire extinguisher
4. Finally, your brain connects these different activations to form a rich understanding

Why This Is Special

This multi-region activation offers a more detailed and nuanced understanding. It's like the difference between reading a dry description of a place and actually experiencing it with all your senses.

The "Aha!" Moment

When a metaphor clicks, you experience a moment of insight—a satisfying feeling of suddenly understanding something complex. This happens because your brain effectively connects the unfamiliar concept to something you already know well.

Your brain rewards this connection with a small release of feel-good chemicals, which is why good metaphors often feel satisfying.

Speed vs. Depth

Interestingly, your brain sometimes takes a little longer to process metaphors than literal language. However, this extra effort leads to a deeper understanding and better memory.

It's like the difference between quickly skimming a text (faster but shallower) and reading it carefully (slightly slower but much deeper).

Why This Matters for Healthcare

In healthcare communication, this deeper processing is highly valuable. When patients understand their condition or treatment through well-chosen metaphors, they aren't just receiving information - they're creating a mental model they can use to understand their health situation.

This neural response to metaphors explains why people often say, "Now I get it!" when a doctor finally uses a clear metaphor to clarify a complex medical concept.

Memory Formation and Retention Through Metaphor

How Metaphors Help Us Remember

When you hear something like "This medication is like a bouncer at a club, keeping the bad elements out," your brain does something special. Instead of just storing the words, it forms a mental image and links it to experiences you already have.

Why This Sticks Better

Consider how difficult it is to recall a string of technical terms compared to remembering a story or an image. There are several reasons why metaphors tend to create stronger memories.

1. **Double Coding:** Metaphors are stored in two ways - as words and as images or experiences. This provides your brain with multiple pathways to recall the information later.
2. **Emotional Hooks:** Metaphors often relate to things with emotional significance. When your doctor says a medication "works like a shield," it appeals to feelings of protection and safety. Emotions serve as memory glue.
3. **Familiar Frameworks:** Your brain loves connecting new information to what you already know. When medication instructions use a metaphor like "think of this like setting your alarm clock," your brain attaches the new info to existing knowledge about alarm clocks.

The Practical Impact

In healthcare settings, this memory advantage is huge:

- Patients remember their medication instructions better when they're explained through familiar metaphors
- Complex conditions are easier to understand and remember when explained with relatable comparisons.
- Treatment benefits stay in memory when linked to everyday experiences

Real-World Results

Studies show that patients who receive information through suitable metaphors usually:

- Remember more key points about their treatment
- Recall information more accurately weeks or months later
- Can better explain their condition to others

This occurs because metaphors turn abstract medical ideas into concrete, memorable mental images that the brain naturally remembers, making metaphors not just artistic language but effective tools for helping important health information stay with people when they need it.

Emotional Engagement and Decision-Making

How Emotions Drive Our Choices

Most of us like to believe we make decisions based solely on facts and logic. However, the reality is that our emotions significantly influence every choice we make, especially when it comes to our health.

Why Metaphors Tap Into Feelings

Metaphors link dry facts to feelings we understand. When a doctor describes a medication as "a shield protecting your cells," it not only explains its function but also makes you feel protected and safe.

These emotional responses happen almost immediately, often before our logical brain fully processes the information.

The Power of Feeling and Knowing

When we understand something both intellectually AND emotionally:

1. We pay more attention to it
2. We remember it better
3. We feel more confident in our decisions about it
4. We're more likely to take action

How This Works in Healthcare Decisions

Let's say you need to decide between two treatments:

- Treatment A is described using technical terms about efficacy rates
- Treatment B is described as "working like a smart key that unlocks only the doors you need to open."

Most people feel more emotionally connected to the second description. Even if both treatments work equally well, the metaphor offers a sense of comfort and confidence that can influence the decision.

Beyond Just Positive Emotions

Good metaphors not only evoke positive feelings, but also aid people in confronting difficult realities.

A metaphor like "treatment is a marathon, not a sprint" doesn't sugarcoat the challenges ahead, but it offers an emotional framework for understanding and accepting them.

The Brain Science Behind It

When we make decisions, our brain processes information from both emotional centers, like the amygdala, and logical centers, like the prefrontal cortex. Metaphors effectively address both parts of this decision-making system.

This is why well-crafted metaphors in pharmaceutical marketing not only inform people but also help them feel confident in making healthcare decisions that might otherwise seem overwhelming or confusing.

PART II: STRATEGIC APPLICATIONS IN PHARMA

Part II

Strategic Applications in Pharma

Making Metaphors Work in the Real World

This section of the book explores the theory of metaphors and shows how to apply it practically, especially in pharmaceutical marketing.

Customizing for Different Audiences

Just as you wouldn't speak to your doctor the same way you would to your grandmother, pharmaceutical metaphors need to be customized for different groups.

- For doctors and nurses, metaphors can serve as shortcuts for explaining complex mechanisms to patients.
- For patients, metaphors can help make treatment instructions and benefits easier to understand.
- For insurance companies and decision-makers, metaphors help convey value in understandable terms

Adapting for Different Health Conditions

Different health conditions need different metaphor approaches:

- Chronic conditions fit well with journey and management metaphors ("diabetes management is like balancing a seesaw").
- Cancer treatments benefit from precise metaphors instead of just battle language ("targeted therapy is like a smart missile").
- Mental health needs metaphors that reduce stigma and normalize experiences
- Rare diseases need metaphors that make invisible conditions visible to others

Explaining How Drugs Work

One of the biggest challenges in the pharmaceutical industry is explaining how medicines work in the body. This section demonstrates how to:

- Turn molecular processes into visual stories anyone can understand
- Create metaphors that accurately represent biological processes without oversimplification
- Develop consistent metaphor systems across marketing materials

These practical applications show how to go beyond theory and develop metaphors that work well in the complex world of pharmaceutical marketing. Instead of just creative exercises, these methods are strategic tools that address specific communication challenges in healthcare.

Chapter Four

Stakeholder Analysis: Tailoring Metaphors to Different Audiences

Why One Size Doesn't Fit All

Different people involved in healthcare decisions need information presented in different ways. A metaphor that works for a doctor might confuse a patient, while one that resonates with patients might seem too simple for insurance companies.

For Healthcare Professionals

Doctors, nurses, and pharmacists already understand medical terminology but need effective ways to explain concepts to patients. For them, metaphors should:

- Provide communication shortcuts they can reuse with patients
- Balance accuracy with simplicity
- Respect their medical knowledge while giving them new language tools

Example: Instead of merely stating that a medication is an "IL-6 inhibitor," use a metaphorical description, such as "a circuit breaker that interrupts the inflammatory messaging system."

For Patients and Caregivers

Patients need metaphors that link medical concepts to everyday experiences they recognize. For them, metaphors should:

- Use familiar, everyday references
- Create clear mental pictures
- Avoid frightening or negative associations where possible
- Help explain why treatments are necessary

Example: Describing cholesterol medication as "like a drain cleaner that helps keep your pipes from getting clogged" relates to familiar household experiences.

For Payers and Decision-Makers

Insurance companies and healthcare system administrators focus on value, outcomes, and the impact on the system. Their metaphors should:

- Emphasize return on investment
- Illustrate long-term benefits
- Connect to business and economic concepts they understand
- Show system-wide impacts

Example: Presenting a preventative medication as "an investment that pays dividends by preventing costly hospitalizations" speaks their language.

By understanding what matters to each stakeholder group and finding metaphors that connect with their existing knowledge and priorities, pharmaceutical marketers can communicate more effectively with everyone involved in healthcare decisions. The right metaphor doesn't just clarify—it directly addresses what each audience cares about most.

Healthcare Professionals: Speaking Their Language

What Makes Healthcare Professionals Different

Doctors, nurses, and pharmacists already understand medical terminology—they don't need simplified explanations of basic concepts. What they require are effective ways to communicate with patients and efficient methods to understand new information.

Bridging Two Worlds

Healthcare professionals operate in two spheres - the technical realm of medicine and the daily world of patient care. Effective metaphors aid them in connecting these spheres by:

- Respecting their expertise while giving them new communication tools
- Providing language shortcuts they can use with patients
- Balancing scientific accuracy with accessibility

What Works With This Audience

For healthcare professionals, the most effective metaphors include:

1. **Acknowledge their expertise**: Begin with the science, then introduce the metaphor as a communication tool.
2. **Maintain accuracy**: Avoid metaphors that oversimplify and could be misleading.
3. **Focus on patient conversations**: Use metaphors to enhance patient understanding.
4. **Save time**: Use metaphors as quick and effective ways to explain complex ideas.

Practical Examples

Instead of just saying a biologic "blocks TNF-alpha receptors," compare it to "acting like a key that fits into a specific lock, preventing the inflammatory cascade from being triggered."

For a complex treatment plan, consider comparing it to "training for a marathon with different phases and support systems" as a way to explain the treatment journey to patients.

The Benefit to Healthcare Professionals

When given effective metaphors, healthcare professionals can:

- Explain treatments more clearly in limited appointment times
- Improve patient understanding and treatment adherence
- Communicate complex benefits and risks in memorable ways

Healthcare professionals don't need metaphors to understand medicine themselves, but they highly value metaphors that help them communicate medicine effectively to others.

Patients and Caregivers: Making the Complex Accessible

Meeting People Where They Are

Patients and caregivers often lack medical knowledge. They encounter unfamiliar terms, hidden processes inside the body, and often experience emotional stress related to health issues. They need metaphors that connect to their everyday lives.

What Works for Patients and Caregivers

For this audience, effective metaphors:

1. **Use everyday references**: Relate medical concepts to common experiences like driving a car, cooking, or gardening.
2. **Create clear mental pictures**: Help them visualize what's happening inside the body.
3. **Acknowledge emotions**: Recognize the fear, hope, or frustration often associated with health challenges.
4. **Empower understanding**: Provide them with a framework to understand their condition and treatment.

Real-Life Examples That Work

Instead of describing a medication as "an anti-inflammatory that reduces cytokine production," patients connect better with: "This medication works like a traffic officer that directs inflammation away from your joints."

Instead of explaining "glucose regulation," diabetes management becomes clearer with: "Think of managing diabetes like balancing a seesaw - food raises your blood sugar on one side, while insulin and exercise lower it on the other."

Beyond Just Understanding

Good metaphors for patients not only foster understanding -- they also support:

- Better treatment adherence because patients grasp why medications matter
- More productive conversations with healthcare providers
- Ability to explain their condition to family and friends
- Reduced anxiety that comes from making the unknown known

Simple Without Being Simplistic

The main challenge is making complex information understandable without talking down to patients. Effective metaphors respect patients' intelligence while recognizing their lack of specialized knowledge. They turn medical complexity into familiar ideas without losing the important meaning patients need to make informed decisions about their care.

Payers and Decision-Makers: Value Communication

What Makes This Audience Different

Payers and healthcare decision-makers (insurance companies, hospital administrators, formulary committees) mainly focus on costs, outcomes, and system-wide effects. They analyze how medications fit into the larger healthcare economic picture.

Speaking Their Language

For this audience, impactful metaphors:

1. **Connect to business concepts**: Use comparisons to investments, insurance, and resource management
2. **Illustrate long-term value**: Show how upfront costs lead to downstream savings
3. **Demonstrate systems thinking**: Describe how a treatment impacts the whole healthcare system.
4. **Quantify abstract benefits**: Make intangible values more concrete

Examples That Resonate

Instead of just presenting statistics about a preventative medication, use a metaphor like: "This treatment works like a flood barrier - there's an upfront investment, but it prevents much costlier damage down the road."

To explain value beyond direct medical costs: "This therapy is like upgrading from basic transportation to a reliable vehicle - the initial cost is higher, but you save on maintenance, avoid breakdowns, and improve productivity."

From Numbers to Narratives

Payers are accustomed to viewing data and spreadsheets. Metaphors help turn these numbers into compelling stories about value.

- How preventing complications is like preventative maintenance
- How improved quality of life translate to workforce productivity
- How new treatment paradigms create ripple effects throughout the system

Building Economic Arguments

The right metaphors help shape economic arguments in ways that relate to how decision-makers already perceive value. Instead of relying only on clinical data, metaphors demonstrate why a treatment is economically sensible within the larger healthcare system.

Effective value communication uses metaphors that respect payers' financial focus while helping them see beyond immediate costs to the overall picture of a treatment's economic impact.

Chapter Five

Disease-Specific Metaphor Strategies

Why Different Conditions Need Different Approaches

Just as you wouldn't use the same language to describe a headache and a broken bone, different health conditions require different metaphor approaches. The best metaphors match the nature of the condition they describe.

Chronic Conditions: Journey and Management Metaphors

Chronic conditions like diabetes, arthritis, or hypertension last for years or a lifetime. For these, the most effective metaphors focus on:

- **Long-term journeys**: "Managing diabetes is like taking a cross-country road trip - you need to check your gauges regularly and adjust as needed."
- **Balance and maintenance**: "Think of arthritis management as tending a garden - regular care prevents problems from growing out of control."

These metaphors assist patients in accepting the ongoing nature of their condition while highlighting their active role in managing it.

Oncology: Beyond Battle Metaphors

Cancer has traditionally been described using war metaphors ("fighting cancer," "battling the disease"). While these resonate with some patients, others require different approaches.

- **Precision targeting**: "This targeted therapy works like a smart key that only unlocks certain cells."
- **Restoration metaphors**: "Immunotherapy helps restore your body's natural security system so it can recognize and remove cancer cells."

These alternatives offer hope without putting pressure on patients to constantly "fight" or implying they've "lost the battle" if treatment isn't successful.

Mental Health: Breaking Stigma Through New Metaphors

Mental health conditions improve when metaphors normalize experiences and lessen shame.

- **Weather patterns**: "Depression is like weather, not a personal failing - sometimes there are storms, but they do pass."
- **Circuit and connection metaphors**: "Anxiety can be like having an overactive alarm system that rings even when there's no danger."

These help steer clear of metaphors that suggest character flaws.

Rare Diseases: Bringing the Invisible into View

Rare diseases often struggle with recognition and a lack of understanding. Their metaphors need to:

- **Create visibility**: "Though you can't see it, this condition is like having your body's assembly line missing a critical worker."
- **Explain impact**: "Imagine trying to drive a car where the gas and brake pedals work unpredictably - that's what living with this condition feels like."

These help patients describe their unseen experiences to others.

Matching the metaphor strategy to the specific disease fosters more resonant, effective communication that genuinely addresses the needs of each patient group.

Chronic Conditions: Journey and Management Metaphors

Why Journey Metaphors Work for Chronic Conditions

Chronic conditions like diabetes, arthritis, or heart disease persist with people for years or even a lifetime. Journey metaphors are effective because they:

- Acknowledge that managing the condition is an ongoing process
- Recognize that there will be ups and downs along the way
- Emphasize that patients are active participants, not passive victims
- Set realistic expectations for the long-term nature of treatment

Examples of Effective Journey Metaphors

- **The Road Trip**: "Managing diabetes is like taking a long road trip. You need to check your gauges (blood sugar) regularly, adjust your speed (medication) as needed, and sometimes take detours (handle unexpected situations). The journey continues, but you're in the driver's seat."
- **The Marathon**: "Treating a chronic condition isn't a sprint—it's more like a marathon. Pace yourself, build your support team, celebrate milestones along the way, and remember that steady progress matters more than speed."

Management Metaphors That Resonate

Management metaphors emphasize the ongoing balance and maintenance required.

- **The Garden**: "Think of managing arthritis like tending a garden. Daily care (medication, gentle exercise) prevents weeds (flare-ups) from taking over. Some seasons are easier than others, but consistent attention keeps things flourishing."
- **The Thermostat**: "Your treatment plan works like a thermostat, not an on/off switch. It's about finding the right settings that keep your condition regulated within a comfortable range, with occasional adjustments as needed."

Why These Work Better Than Other Approaches

These metaphors are more effective than crisis or battle metaphors because they:

- Set realistic expectations for managing the condition long-term.

- Empower patients instead of making them feel like victims
- Recognize that perfect control isn't always achievable.
- Normalize the ups and downs of chronic condition management

Effective metaphors help patients accept their condition without being defined by it and empower them to take an active role in managing their health without feeling overwhelmed by its lifelong nature.

Oncology: Battle Metaphors and Alternatives

Why Battle Metaphors Are Widespread

For decades, we've talked about cancer using war language:

- "Fighting cancer"
- "Battling the disease"
- "Weapons against cancer"
- "Winning the war on cancer"

These metaphors gained popularity because they highlight determination and rally support. They can help some patients feel empowered and prepared to face their diagnosis.

The Drawbacks of Battle Language

However, battle metaphors can cause issues:

- They can make patients feel like failures if treatment isn't successful ("lost the battle")
- They put pressure on patients to always be "brave fighters" even when they're exhausted
- They focus on aggression when sometimes gentler approaches are needed
- They can increase anxiety by framing everything as a life-or-death struggle

Alternative Metaphors That Work Well

Here are various ways to discuss cancer that many patients find useful:

- **Journey Metaphors**: "Cancer treatment is a path with different stages. Each person's route is unique, with support available along the way."
- **Restoration Metaphors**: "Immunotherapy helps restore your body's natural security system so it can recognize and remove cancer cells that shouldn't be there."
- **Precision Metaphors**: "This targeted therapy works like a smart key that only affects specific locks, leaving healthy cells alone."
- **Balance Metaphors**: "Treatment is about creating an environment in your body where cancer cells struggle while healthy cells thrive."

Choosing What Works for Each Patient

The most effective way is to tailor metaphors to each patient.

- Some find strength in battle language
- Others prefer journey metaphors that acknowledge ups and downs
- Some connect with gardening or weather metaphors
- Many respond to technology or tool-based comparisons

The goal is to find language that helps patients understand their treatment while supporting their emotional well-being during a challenging time. The right metaphor can provide both clarity and comfort.

Mental Health: Breaking Stigma Through New Metaphors

The Power of Better Language

The words we use to describe mental health conditions can either foster understanding or increase shame. Traditional metaphors often worsened the situation by suggesting personal weakness or character flaws. New metaphors are transforming this.

Moving Beyond Harmful Comparisons

Old metaphors that increased stigma included language about:

- "Broken" minds
- "Weak" character
- "Unbalanced" personalities
- Being "crazy" or "insane"

These comparisons indicated that there was a fundamental issue with the person, instead of identifying a health condition.

Helpful New Metaphors

Here are better ways to talk about mental health conditions:

- **Weather Patterns**: "Depression is like weather, not a personal failing. Sometimes there are storms, sunny days, or fog. The weather isn't your fault, but you can learn to prepare for different conditions."
- **Circuit and Connection Metaphors**: "Anxiety can be like having an overactive alarm system that rings even when there's no real danger. Treatment helps recalibrate this system to respond appropriately."
- **Brain Chemistry**: "Mental health conditions are like having different levels of brain chemicals, similar to how some people have different levels of insulin. Medication helps adjust these levels."
- **Operating System**: "Sometimes your brain's operating system needs updates or troubleshooting, just like a computer. Therapy is like running those updates."

Why These New Metaphors Help

These newer metaphors help lessen stigma because they:

1. Separate the person from the condition
2. Normalize mental health as a health issue, not a character issue
3. Focus on management rather than "fixing" something "broken"
4. Create language that makes it easier to ask for help

Real Impact on People's Lives

When we alter our metaphors for mental health, people tend to feel more comfortable.

- Discussing their experiences openly
- Seeking treatment earlier
- Maintaining treatment longer
- Supporting others with similar conditions

The right metaphors don't just change how we talk about mental health - they change how we think about it, helping to create a society where mental health is treated with the same understanding and compassion as physical health.

Rare Diseases: Making the Invisible Visible

The Double Challenge of Rare Conditions

People with rare diseases face two major problems: not only do they have serious medical conditions, but often nobody can "see" what they're experiencing. Many rare diseases lack obvious external signs, leading to comments like "but you don't look sick."

Why Metaphors Are Especially Important

For rare diseases, good metaphors serve critical purposes:

- Help patients explain their invisible experiences to others
- Create understanding where medical terms fail
- Build empathy for symptoms others can't see
- Help patients feel less isolated in their experience

Metaphors That Make the Invisible Visible

- **The Missing Worker**: "Though you can't see it, this condition is like having your body's assembly line missing a critical worker. Everything slows down, and certain products never get made properly."
- **The Electrical System**: "Imagine your body's wiring has some frayed connections. Sometimes everything works fine, but other times you get unexpected outages or power surges in random systems."
- **The Unpredictable Car**: "Living with this condition is like driving a car where the gas and brake pedals work unpredictably - sometimes responding normally, sometimes not responding at all, and sometimes activating without being pressed."

Creating Community Understanding

Good metaphors help build connections between people with rare conditions and those around them.

- They give family members language to understand the experience
- They help doctors without specialist knowledge grasp the patient experience
- They provide ways for patients to explain workplace accommodations they need
- They build public awareness that influences research funding

From Isolation to Connection

When someone can finally say, "it's like trying to run a marathon while wearing heavy weights that nobody else can see," and be understood, it transforms their experience. The right metaphors don't just clarify rare diseases - they help make the invisible experience visible to everyone, building a connection where there was once isolation.

Chapter Six

Mechanism of Action: Visualizing the Invisible

The Challenge of Explaining How Medicines Work

One of the hardest things to explain about medications is how they work inside the body. These processes:

- Happen at a microscopic level, we can't see
- Involve complex chemistry and biology
- Use technical terms that most people don't know
- Take place through multiple steps

This is where good metaphors become essential; they make invisible processes visible.

Turning Molecules into Mental Pictures

Instead of discussing "enzyme inhibition" or "receptor antagonists," effective metaphors build clear mental images.

- **The Lock and Key**: "This medication works like a key that fits into a specific lock on your cells. When it turns the lock, it activates processes that reduce inflammation."
- **The Blocker**: "Think of this drug as a bouncer at a club door. It stands in front of certain receptors and prevents harmful substances from getting in and causing trouble."
- **The Messenger**: "This medicine acts like a message carrier, delivering instructions to your cells that tell them to produce substances that help heal damaged tissue."

Helping People See Complex Processes

Good mechanism metaphors break down complicated multi-step processes into understandable sequences:

- **The Assembly Line**: "Your immune system is like a factory with an assembly line that produces antibodies. This medication helps speed up production when you have an infection."
- **The Traffic System**: "Blood clotting is like a traffic system with signals. This medication works as a traffic officer, keeping blood flowing smoothly without unnecessary stops (clots)."

Why This Matters to Patients

When patients can visualize how their medicine works, they:

Feel more confident in their treatment

- Understand why timing or consistency matters
- Can better explain their medication to others
- Often show better adherence to treatment plans

Effective visual metaphors turn mysterious pills into clear tools, enabling patients to take an active role in their treatment instead of just passively taking medicine.

Translating Molecular Processes into Comprehensible Images

Making the Tiny World Make Sense

Molecular processes occur at a scale so small that we can't see them with our naked eyes. Even with powerful microscopes, we often can't observe these processes in real-time. However, patients and healthcare stakeholders need to understand what is happening.

Starting with Familiar Objects

Good metaphors translate molecular activities into everyday objects people already understand:

Keys and Locks: "This medication is shaped exactly like a key that fits into a specific lock on your cells. When other substances try to open that lock and cause inflammation, this medicine blocks the keyhole so they can't get in."

Puzzle Pieces: "Your body's enzymes and proteins fit together like puzzle pieces. This medicine mimics one of those pieces, taking its place in the puzzle but changing how the finished picture works."

Switches and Dimmers: "Think of this biologic as operating the dimmer switch on your immune system. Instead of turning it fully off (which would be dangerous), it adjusts the intensity to a more appropriate level."

Creating Motion and Action

Molecular processes are dynamic, not static. Effective metaphors capture this movement:

Conveyor Belts: "Your cells have tiny conveyor belts that move materials from one part to another. This medication influences how quickly certain conveyor belts operate."

Mail Delivery: "Hormones are like mail carriers delivering important messages throughout your body. This medication ensures the right messages get delivered to the right cells."

Making Complexity Manageable

Rather than explaining every molecular detail, good visual metaphors focus on the key actions that matter:

Traffic Signals: "Instead of explaining all the chemistry of blood clotting, we can describe anti-coagulants as traffic officers keeping blood flowing smoothly through your vessels."

Filtering Systems: "Medications that affect kidney function can be described as adjusting the body's filtering system - making the filters more or less permeable to certain substances."

These visual comparisons transform abstract molecular processes into concrete images people can picture in their minds. This makes a significant difference in understanding how medications work in the body and why taking them correctly is important.

Personifying Biological Processes

Giving Human Traits to Body Systems

One effective way to explain complex biology is by attributing human qualities to cells, proteins, and other bodily components. This approach transforms abstract processes into relatable stories with characters that people can connect with.

How It Works in Practice

Instead of describing technical processes, we create characters and stories:

Immune Cells as Security Guards: "Your white blood cells work like security guards patrolling your body. They're trained to spot intruders (bacteria, viruses) and either capture them or call for backup when needed."

Enzymes as Workers: "Think of enzymes as specialized workers in your body's factory. Each has a specific job - some are like scissors cutting things apart, others are like assembly workers putting molecules together."

Hormones as Messengers: "Hormones are like messengers running through your bloodstream delivering important notes to different organs. Insulin is a messenger that tells cells to open their doors and let sugar in."

Why This Approach Is Effective

Personification works particularly well because:

1. **It creates clear roles and purposes** - People understand what security guards do more easily than what "phagocytes" do
2. **It establishes relationships** - We can explain how different parts of the body communicate and work together
3. **It adds emotion and motivation** - Characters have reasons for their actions, making processes more memorable
4. **It simplifies without oversimplifying** - Complex interactions become understandable stories

Examples in Pharmaceutical Marketing

In medication explanations, personification helps explain how treatments work:

- "This antibiotic works like a saboteur that prevents bacteria from building their protective walls, making them vulnerable."
- "This pain medication acts like a gatekeeper that prevents pain signals from being delivered to your brain."
- "This cholesterol medication works like a cleanup crew that helps remove excess cholesterol from your bloodstream."

By turning body processes into characters with specific roles, personification helps people form clear mental images of what is happening inside their bodies and how medications help these processes work more effectively.

Case Study: Evolution of Immune System Metaphors

How We've Described the Immune System Over Time

The way we discuss the immune system has undergone significant changes over the years, reflecting both our evolving scientific understanding and shifting cultural perspectives.

The Military Metaphors: 1950s-1990s

For decades, we primarily described the immune system using war and military language:

- Immune cells "attack" invaders
- The body "defends" against pathogens
- Vaccines "arm" the immune system
- The body "fights off" infection

These metaphors emerged during the Cold War era and reflected the militaristic thinking of the time. They were straightforward but often oversimplified the immune response as purely aggressive.

The Security System Update: 1990s-2010s

As our understanding grew more sophisticated, so did our metaphors:

- Immune cells became "security guards" that patrol and check ID
- The immune system became an "intelligent security network" with surveillance
- Recognition processes were described as "scanning for threats."
- Immune tolerance was explained as "approving authorized visitors."

This shift acknowledged that the immune system doesn't just attack—it actively monitors, identifies, and makes decisions about what belongs and what doesn't.

The Modern Ecological Approach: 2010s-Present

Today's most advanced immune metaphors use ecological and network concepts:

- The immune system as an "ecosystem" with different players in balance
- Immune regulation as "maintaining homeostasis" rather than just fighting

- Microbiome interactions described as "community management."
- Autoimmunity explained as "mistaken identity" rather than "friendly fire."

Why This Evolution Matters

These changing metaphors have had real impacts on how patients understand treatments:

- Older patients treated with early immunosuppressants were told their "defenses were being weakened."
- Patients today receiving modern immunotherapies hear that their "immune system is being retrained" or "recalibrated."

The newer metaphors better explain complex immunotherapies, such as checkpoint inhibitors and selective immune modulators, which don't just boost or suppress immunity, but instead modify specific pathways.

This evolution demonstrates how metaphors are more than just creative language—they embody our scientific understanding and influence how patients grasp their treatments. The right metaphor can turn a complex biological process into something patients can visualize and comprehend.

PART III: IMPLEMENTATION AND BEST PRACTICES

Part III

Implementation and Best Practices

Putting Metaphors to Work in the Real World

This section of the book moves from theory to practical application, offering specific methods to create, test, and effectively utilize metaphors in your pharmaceutical marketing.

Creating Metaphors That Work

Instead of just hoping for creative inspiration, this section provides step-by-step methods for developing effective metaphors.

- Research techniques to understand your audience's existing knowledge
- Methods for testing metaphors with target groups before full implementation
- Frameworks for ensuring metaphors are both accurate and accessible
- Practical worksheets and exercises to generate metaphor options

Digital Era Considerations

Today's marketing occurs across multiple channels, particularly digital ones. This section covers:

- How to adapt metaphors for different platforms (social media, websites, apps)
- Creating interactive metaphors that engage people digitally
- Using visualization tools to bring metaphors to life
- How AR/VR technologies are creating new possibilities for metaphor expression

Ethical Guardrails

Metaphors are powerful, which means they must be used responsibly. This section addresses:

- How to avoid metaphors that might mislead or overpromise
- Cultural considerations when using metaphors in global markets
- Balancing hope and optimism with realistic expectations
- Regulatory considerations when using metaphors in regulated communications

These practical guidelines assist marketing teams in implementing metaphors effectively and responsibly. Instead of just understanding metaphors in theory, readers gain tangible tools to apply them in ways that truly connect with healthcare stakeholders while upholding ethical standards.

Chapter Seven

Developing Effective Metaphors: A Practical Guide

Step 1: Know Your Audience First

Before creating any metaphors, understand who you're talking to:

- What is their existing knowledge level?
- What everyday experiences are familiar to them?
- What are their concerns and priorities?
- What cultural references would resonate with them?

For example, for patients with diabetes, find out what aspects of management they struggle with most before choosing your metaphors.

Step 2: Clarify What Needs Explaining

Identify exactly what complex concept needs to be made simpler:

- Is it how a medication works?
- Is it why adherence matters?
- Is it a complex biological process?
- Is it the treatment journey?

Be specific about what you want your metaphor to accomplish.

Step 3: Brainstorm Potential Comparisons

Generate multiple options by asking:

- What everyday objects work similarly?
- What processes follow a similar pattern?
- What relationships mirror this interaction?
- What stories have a similar structure?

For example, when explaining how a selective medication works, you might brainstorm ideas like keys and locks, puzzle pieces, light switches, or mail carriers with specific addresses.

Step 4: Test With Real People

Before fully committing to a metaphor:

- Try it out with members of your target audience
- Ask what they understand from the metaphor
- Check for any unintended interpretations
- See if it creates the "aha!" moment you're seeking

Be prepared to refine or abandon metaphors that don't connect.

Step 5: Refine For Accuracy and Clarity

Fine-tune your metaphor to ensure it:

- Accurately represents the key aspects of what you're explaining
- Doesn't create misleading impressions
- Is concise and clear
- Balances simplicity with necessary complexity

Step 6: Implement Across Channels

Adapt your metaphor for different contexts:

- How will it work visually versus in text?
- How can it be abbreviated for space-limited channels?
- How might it be expanded for educational materials?
- How can it be consistent across different touchpoints?

Following this practical process helps ensure that your metaphors are not only creative but also genuinely effective in helping your audience understand complex pharmaceutical concepts in an accessible way.

Research Methods for Metaphor Development

Understanding Your Audience First

Before creating metaphors, you must grasp how your audience thinks:

In-depth interviews help you understand how patients or healthcare professionals discuss their conditions or treatments. Listen for metaphors they use naturally - these often serve as great starting points.

Focus groups can uncover shared understandings and common points of reference. When someone says, "It feels like..." or "It's similar to...", they're providing valuable metaphor seeds.

Observational research in clinical settings reveals how doctors currently explain concepts to patients. Watch for moments when understanding occurs—what comparison made that happen?

Finding What Resonates

Once you have potential metaphors, test them:

Comprehension testing asks people to explain back what they understand from a metaphor. This quickly reveals if your comparison creates the right mental model.

A/B testing with various metaphors reveals which ones result in clearer understanding or more intense emotional reactions. Try explaining the same idea using different metaphors and see which one proves more effective.

Metaphor mapping exercises ask participants to draw connections between the metaphor and the actual concept it represents. The thoroughness of their maps shows how well the metaphor works.

Practical Tools That Work

Simple research techniques yield powerful insights:

Word association tests reveal what concepts naturally connect in people's minds. Ask "What does 'immune system' make you think of" to find natural metaphor connections.

"Explain it to a child" exercises force participants to use simple comparisons to explain complex topics, generating metaphor ideas.

Cultural reference scanning identifies popular concepts that can serve as metaphors across your target audience, ranging from sports to cooking to technology.

These research methods don't need huge budgets but do require listening carefully to how people naturally think about and explain complex health topics. The best metaphors often come from this research rather than from creative brainstorming in isolation.

Testing and Refining Metaphors with Target Audiences

Why Testing Matters

Even metaphors that sound perfect in a marketing meeting can fail in the real world. Testing with actual target audiences helps you discover:

- If people understand what you intended
- If the metaphor creates any confusion
- If it connects emotionally
- If it helps people remember key information

Simple Ways to Test Metaphors

You don't need complex research to test metaphors effectively:

The "Explain Back" Method: After sharing your metaphor, ask people to explain the concept back to you in their own words. This quickly reveals if they've grasped the right idea or misunderstood something.

Preference Testing: Show people different metaphor options for the same concept and ask which one makes more sense to them and why. This often reveals surprising preferences.

Visual Association: Ask people what image comes to mind when they hear your metaphor. If their mental picture matches your intention, you're on the right track.

Refining Based on Feedback

When testing reveals problems, don't just start over - refine strategically:

1. **Adjust the complexity:** Sometimes you need to simplify further; other times you need to add a bit more detail.
2. **Change the reference point:** If your audience doesn't connect with your comparison (such as sports references for non-sports fans), consider a more universal experience.
3. **Address misconceptions directly:** If testing shows a specific misunderstanding, modify your metaphor to counter that confusion specifically.

Real-World Examples

A pharmaceutical company discovered that their "lock and key" metaphor for a receptor antagonist confused patients because they believed the drug "unlocked" something positive. By switching to a "protective shield" metaphor instead, understanding improved significantly.

Another company found that their "traffic cop" metaphor for a blood thinner worked well with older patients, but younger patients better understood the "filtering system" metaphor. They adjusted their materials for different age groups accordingly.

Testing isn't just a final check—it's a crucial part of developing metaphors that often results in the most effective comparisons.

Implementation Across Communication Channels

Making Metaphors Work Everywhere

Once you have effective metaphors, you need to use them consistently across all the ways you communicate with your audience. Here's how to adapt your metaphors for different channels:

Print Materials and Brochures

In print, you have space to develop your metaphors fully:

- Use visuals that reinforce your comparison
- Include slightly more detailed explanations
- Consider using a series of images that show a process
- Make sure text and visuals work together to reinforce the same metaphor

For example, if using a "key and lock" metaphor, show an actual visual sequence of the key finding and fitting the right lock.

Digital Websites and Apps

Digital channels allow for interactive metaphors:

- Use animations to show processes over time
- Consider interactive elements that let users explore the metaphor
- Break complex metaphors into digestible sections
- Use progressive disclosure to reveal more details as users engage

For example, an interactive body map might let users "zoom in" to see how a medication works at different levels.

Social Media and Short-Form Content

On channels with limited space or attention spans:

- Focus on the core comparison without all the details
- Use striking visuals that instantly communicate the metaphor
- Consider short animations or GIFs that show key aspects
- Use consistent hashtags that reinforce your metaphor

Healthcare Professional Materials

For medical professionals, you can add more layers:

- Connect the metaphor to the scientific mechanism
- Provide both simple and more detailed versions for patient communication
- Include research that validates your approach
- Offer communication tools based on your metaphor

Face-to-Face Communications

For sales representatives or medical science liaisons:

- Provide physical props or demonstrations that bring metaphors to life
- Train on how to adjust the metaphor for different audiences
- Develop answers to common questions about the comparison
- Create conversation guides that help introduce metaphors naturally.

The key is maintaining consistency across all these channels so your audience receives the same core message regardless of where they encounter it, while tailoring the presentation to suit each channel's unique strengths.

Chapter Eight

Digital Transformation of Metaphor Usage

How Digital Tools Have Changed Metaphors

The digital revolution has changed how we create and use metaphors in pharmaceutical marketing. Instead of only static images and text descriptions, we now have many more ways to animate metaphors.

Interactive and Dynamic Metaphors

Digital platforms allow metaphors to become interactive experiences:

- **Animated Sequences:** Rather than just describing how a medication works as a "key in a lock," you can show the entire process of the key finding, fitting, and turning in the lock.
- **User-Controlled Exploration:** Apps and websites let patients zoom in and out of body systems or toggle between different views of the same process.
- **Progressive Disclosure:** Digital tools can reveal metaphors in layers, starting with a simple comparison and adding details as users want to learn more.

For example, a diabetes management app might use a balancing scale metaphor that tips and adjusts as patients enter their food intake and activity levels.

Social Media and Metaphor Virality

Social media has changed how metaphors spread and evolve:

- **Bite-sized Metaphors:** Complex health concepts now need to be explained in short, memorable ways that work in limited character counts.
- **Visual-First Thinking:** Platforms like Instagram and TikTok prioritize visual metaphors that convey meaning instantly, requiring minimal text to communicate their message.

- **Community Adaptation:** Patients now share and modify metaphors among themselves, creating new variations that resonate with their lived experience.

Data Visualization as Metaphor

Modern data tools create new ways to make abstract concepts concrete:

- **Interactive Charts:** Instead of simply stating "your cholesterol is too high," digital tools can visually show a patient's position compared to targets using visual metaphors, such as speedometers or thermometers.
- **Personalized Comparisons:** Digital tools can generate customized visualizations that connect health data to personal references significant to each patient.

Real-time Feedback: Wearable devices use metaphors such as "filling rings" or "climbing stairs" to provide immediate context for abstract health data.

AR/VR Applications

The newest frontier in metaphor development uses augmented and virtual reality:

- **Inside-the-Body Journeys:** VR enables patients to "travel" inside a virtual body to observe how medications work at the cellular level.
- **Overlaid Explanations:** AR can project visual metaphors directly onto real objects, such as illustrating how a patch delivers medication through the skin.
- **Immersive Comparisons:** Virtual reality environments can construct complete metaphorical worlds that aid patients in understanding complex conditions.

These digital transformations have made metaphors more engaging, personalized, and effective at helping people understand complex pharmaceutical concepts.

Interactive and Dynamic Metaphors in Digital Media

Beyond Static Images and Words

Traditional metaphors in print materials were limited to pictures and descriptions that didn't move or change. Digital media has completely transformed this by allowing metaphors to come alive and respond to users in real-time.

How Interactive Metaphors Work

Interactive metaphors let people actively engage rather than just passively read:

- **Touchable Comparisons:** Instead of just seeing a lock and key metaphor for how a drug works, you can drag the key to different locks on a touchscreen and see which one it fits.
- **Adjustable Scenarios:** A blood pressure management app might display a water pipe system, allowing users to adjust lifestyle factors and observe pressure changes in real-time.
- **Explorable Body Systems:** Digital tools enable users to zoom from whole-body views down to cellular levels, with metaphors that adapt at each level—from traffic in blood vessels to keys in locks at the cellular level.

Dynamic Metaphors That Change Over Time

Digital tools also allow metaphors to show change and progression:

- **Treatment Journey Maps:** An interactive path can show the typical progression of treatment, with specific metaphors for each stage that unfold as the user moves through the experience.
- **Before-and-After Comparisons:** Users can slide between views that show conditions with and without treatment, using metaphors that highlight the differences.
- **Real-Time Updates:** Wearable devices utilize metaphors such as "filling a battery" or "watering a plant" to display medication adherence or health progress throughout the day.

Real Examples That Work

A diabetes management app uses a balancing scale that tips in real-time as patients log meals and exercise, making the abstract concept of glucose balance visible and interactive.

An asthma education website features an interactive house where users can click on different triggers (dust, pets, smoke) and observe how they affect animated airways, utilizing a "breathing tube" metaphor that narrows or opens.

These interactive and dynamic approaches help people not just understand health concepts but experience them in ways that create deeper comprehension and more memorable learning.

Social Media and Metaphor Virality

How Social Media Changed Health Metaphors

Social media platforms have transformed the way health metaphors spread and evolve. What once might have been confined to a doctor's office or a brochure can now reach millions of people in just days.

What Makes Metaphors Go Viral

On social media, health metaphors are more likely to spread widely when they:

- **Feel Instantly Relatable:** The "spoon theory" for chronic illness (where energy is measured in spoons) became a sensation because it resonated with people's lived experiences.
- **Use Visual Simplicity:** A comparison showing inflammation as a fire in the body can spread quickly because it creates an immediate visual understanding.
- **Invite Personal Connection:** Metaphors that help people explain their own experiences, such as describing anxiety as "having too many browser tabs open in your brain," tend to be shared more often.
- **Work in Short Form:** The most viral health metaphors can be explained in a single post, image, or short video.

How Patients Have Become Metaphor Creators

One of the biggest changes is that patients now create and spread their own metaphors:

- Chronic illness communities have developed metaphors like "charging batteries" to explain energy management
- Mental health advocates create visual metaphors that help reduce stigma
- Rare disease communities develop metaphors that make invisible symptoms visible to others

The Power of Hashtags and Metaphors

Social media hashtags often center around metaphorical concepts:

- \# SpoonieLife (based on spoon theory)
- \# BrainFog for cognitive symptoms
- \# InvisibleIllness for conditions others can't see

These hashtags create communities around shared metaphorical understanding.

When Healthcare Companies Join The Conversation

Pharmaceutical companies now need to:

- Listen to the metaphors patients are already using
- Engage with community-created comparisons respectfully
- Create metaphors designed to work well in social formats
- Be prepared for how communities might adapt their official metaphors

The most successful companies don't just push their pre-planned metaphors but engage with and learn from the comparisons that naturally emerge and spread among patient communities online.

Data Visualization as Metaphor

Making Numbers Tell Stories

Data visualization turns abstract numbers into visual forms that our brains can understand more easily. These visualizations serve as metaphors, representing one thing (data) through another (shapes, colors, and patterns).

Beyond Just Charts and Graphs

Modern data visualization in healthcare goes beyond basic bar charts:

- **Body Maps:** Rather than displaying numbers for pain levels, an app could present a human figure that patients tap to indicate pain locations, using colors to show intensity
- **Weather Systems:** Some visualizations show health status as weather - sunny days for good readings, storm clouds for concerning ones.
- **Journeys and Paths:** Treatment progress is often represented as a path or road, with milestones indicating significant milestones.

Making the Abstract Concrete

Good health data visualizations make invisible processes visible:

- **Risk Gauges:** Instead of stating someone has a "32% risk of heart disease," a speedometer-like gauge indicates where they fall between low- and high-risk zones.
- **Forest and Trees:** Complex genetic data can be visualized as a forest, where each tree represents a gene or pathway, with size and color indicating its importance.
- **Mountain Climbs:** Achievement of health goals is often visualized as climbing a mountain, with each step representing progress.

Personalized Visual Metaphors

The most effective health visualizations connect to personal meaning:

- **Daily Activities:** Some apps convert step counts into everyday activities, such as "you've walked the equivalent of climbing the Eiffel Tower."
- **Meaningful Comparisons:** Blood sugar levels can be presented in relation to personal targets rather than just as abstract numbers.

- **Growth and Nurturing:** Health improvements are often illustrated through growth metaphors, such as plants developing or gardens flourishing.

These visual metaphors not only display data but also turn numbers into meaningful stories that help patients and healthcare providers understand patterns, make informed decisions, and stay motivated. When someone can literally "see" their health improving through a visual metaphor, it creates understanding that raw numbers alone cannot achieve.

AR/VR Applications in Metaphorical Communication

Taking Metaphors to a New Dimension

Augmented Reality (AR) and Virtual Reality (VR) are revolutionary tools for health metaphors as they allow individuals to experience and engage with metaphorical worlds, rather than merely envisioning them.

Stepping Inside the Body

VR creates immersive experiences that let people:

- **Journey Through Systems:** Instead of just talking about blood cells as "delivery trucks," VR lets patients follow an actual cell, similar to a truck, carrying oxygen through blood vessel "highways."
- **Witness Medication Actions:** Rather than explaining how a drug blocks pain signals, VR can show signals as visible pulses traveling along nerves that are intercepted by medication represented as shields or gates.
- **Experience Size and Scale:** VR helps people understand the microscopic world by allowing them to "shrink down" and see how tiny cellular structures actually are compared to one another.

Overlaying Information on the Real World

AR adds metaphorical elements to what we see in reality:

- **Medication Visualizers:** When a phone is pointed at a pill bottle, AR can display an animation illustrating how the medication works in the body.
- **Treatment Adherence Helpers:** AR apps can display a virtual plant that grows or wilts based on medication adherence, making the abstract concept of consistent treatment more visible.
- **Symptom Communication:** AR tools help patients show doctors exactly what they're experiencing by overlaying visual metaphors onto real body parts.

Real-World Applications That Work

Pain Education: VR programs help chronic pain patients visualize their pain as something they can observe and manage, using metaphors such as pain as a warning light rather than a source of damage.

Phobia Treatment: VR exposure therapy utilizes metaphorical environments to help patients confront their fears in a controlled setting.

Rehabilitation Motivation: AR makes physical therapy more engaging by turning exercises into metaphorical games, like rebuilding a virtual castle through specific movements.

These technologies are powerful because they don't just tell people about metaphors – they allow people to step into them and experience them firsthand. When someone can actually "see" inflammation as a fire in their joints through AR glasses, or "travel" alongside a medication through their bloodstream in VR, understanding reaches a whole new level.

Chapter Nine

Ethical Considerations in Metaphor Selection

Being Powerful Means Being Responsible

Metaphors aren't just creative flourishes - they shape how people understand their health and make decisions. This power comes with ethical responsibilities.

Avoiding Misleading or Oversimplified Representations

Good metaphors simplify without distorting:

- **The Balance Problem:** If you describe a medication as a "shield" against disease, patients might believe they're completely protected when in reality the protection is partial.
- **The Timeline Challenge:** Comparing treatment to a "journey" is helpful, but if the metaphor suggests a clear destination when the condition is chronic, it creates false expectations.
- **The Mechanism Trap:** Explaining that a drug "locks onto" specific receptors is useful, but if it doesn't acknowledge side effects, it's incomplete.

The ethical approach involves creating metaphors that acknowledge limitations while remaining hopeful and clear.

Cultural Sensitivity in Global Marketing

Metaphors that work in one culture may fail or offend in another:

- **Military Metaphors:** "Fighting" disease resonates in some cultures but can pose challenges in societies experiencing recent war trauma.
- **Animal References:** Animals carry various symbolic meanings in different cultures. For example, a metaphor involving owls (which are associated with wisdom in Western cultures) may symbolize death or bad luck in other cultural contexts.

- **Food Comparisons:** When using food-based metaphors, it is crucial to consider religious and cultural food restrictions to avoid alienating your audience.

Ethical metaphor development involves conducting cultural research and local validation before applying it globally.

Balancing Hope with Realism

Perhaps the most delicate ethical balance is between:

- **Encouraging Optimism:** Metaphors should provide hope and motivation for treatment.
- **Preventing False Expectations:** They must not imply guaranteed outcomes or miracle cures.
- **Acknowledging Challenges:** Good metaphors make space for setbacks and difficulties.

For example, instead of describing a cancer treatment as "erasing" cancer cells (which suggests complete elimination), a more ethical metaphor might be "targeting specific cells while sparing healthy ones" (which is hopeful but realistic).

Choosing ethical metaphors emphasizes patient well-being, even when more dramatic or simplified metaphors might seem more appealing from a marketing perspective.

Avoiding Misleading or Oversimplified Representations

The Challenge of Keeping It Simple But Honest

Creating metaphors for healthcare means walking a fine line. You need to make complex science understandable without making promises that the treatment can't keep.

Common Pitfalls to Avoid

The "Magic Bullet" Problem: Describing a medication as a "smart missile" that "targets" only disease cells might make patients think the treatment has no side effects at all. A better way might be to say it is "a treatment that is designed to focus more on problem cells, though it may affect some healthy cells too."

The "Complete Fix" Trap: Saying a medication "repairs" a problem suggests it will fully solve the issue. For chronic conditions, this can give false hope. A more accurate way to describe it might be that it "helps manage" or "works to improve" symptoms.

The "Simple Mechanism" Issue: Explaining that a drug "boosts your immune system" is easy to understand but overlooks the complex ways medications actually work. This can lead to misconceptions about when and how improvement occurs.

Testing for Misconceptions

One practical approach is to ask these questions when creating metaphors:

- Does this metaphor suggest the treatment works faster than it actually does?
- Does it imply a more complete solution than is realistic?
- Does it acknowledge potential limitations or side effects?
- Would a reasonable person develop incorrect expectations from this metaphor?

Real Examples of Better Approaches

Instead of saying an arthritis medication "rebuilds damaged joints" (which suggests complete repair), you might say it "helps support joint health by managing inflammation."

Instead of claiming a cholesterol drug "cleans out your arteries" (implying it removes all buildup), you could describe it as "helping reduce the buildup of cholesterol in blood vessels over time."

The most ethical metaphors help patients understand their treatments while setting realistic expectations about what those treatments can and cannot do. This honesty builds trust and leads to better long-term outcomes, even if it sometimes requires using slightly more complex explanations.

Cultural Sensitivity in Global Marketing

When Metaphors Cross Borders

Metaphors that work perfectly in one country might confuse or even offend people in another. When pharmaceutical marketing goes global, metaphors need careful adaptation.

Watch Out for These Cultural Differences

Different Symbolic Meanings: Colors, animals, and objects hold distinct meanings in various cultures.

- The owl represents wisdom in the West, but death in some parts of Asia
- White symbolizes purity in Western cultures, but mourning in many Eastern cultures
- Hand gestures in visual metaphors can be offensive in some regions

Different Daily Experiences: Metaphors based on local experiences might not translate globally.

- Baseball metaphors ("hitting a home run with treatment") make little sense in countries where baseball isn't popular.
- Traffic metaphors work differently in places with different driving patterns.
- Seasonal metaphors fail when seasons differ across hemispheres.

Health Belief Differences: Cultures have different underlying beliefs about health and illness.

- Battle metaphors ("fighting disease") conflict with harmony-focused health beliefs in some Asian cultures.
- Mechanical metaphors ("body as machine") might clash with more holistic health traditions.
- Control metaphors may not resonate in cultures with more fatalistic views of health.

Practical Approaches That Work

Test Locally: Always check metaphors with people from the target culture before launching them.

Identify Universal Experiences: Focus on shared human experiences that transcend different cultures, such as family relationships, weather patterns, and basic human needs.

Create Adaptable Frameworks: Develop metaphor systems where the core concept works globally, but specific examples can be localized.

Involve Local Teams: Include local marketing teams early in the metaphor development process, not just for translation.

Real-World Example

A pharmaceutical company developed a diabetes management metaphor centered on "balancing scales" rather than using American football or baseball references. The balance concept translated well across cultures while specific visuals were adapted for local contexts, using traditional scales familiar in each region.

Being culturally sensitive isn't just about avoiding offense - it's about creating metaphors that truly resonate with how people understand health in their cultural context.

Balancing Hope with Realism

The Hardest Balance to Strike

Creating metaphors for health conditions and treatments requires careful consideration and thought. People need hope to remain motivated, but false hope can lead to devastating disappointment.

Why This Matters So Much

When patients hear metaphors about their treatment, they form expectations:

- If you describe a cancer treatment as "destroying" cancer cells, they might expect all cancer to disappear
- If you compare a treatment journey to "climbing a mountain," they expect to reach the top
- If you talk about medication "fixing" a problem, they assume a complete solution
- When reality doesn't match these expectations, patients can lose trust and sometimes even abandon treatment.

Finding the Middle Ground

Good metaphors maintain hope while acknowledging reality:

- **Honest About Timelines:** Rather than saying a treatment "quickly resolves" symptoms, a more effective metaphor might be "gradually turns down the volume" on symptoms.
- **Clear About Limitations:** Rather than describing a medication as a "shield" (suggesting complete protection), it might be a "rainfall that helps reduce the fire of inflammation."
- **Open About Uncertainty:** For situations with variable outcomes, metaphors might include natural variations, such as weather patterns, instead of simple on/off switches.

Examples That Strike the Balance

For chronic conditions: "Managing this condition is like tending a garden - with the right care it can flourish, though it will always need attention."

For treatments with partial efficacy: "This medication works like a dimmer switch rather than an on/off button - it can reduce symptoms significantly but typically doesn't eliminate them."

For difficult recovery processes: "Recovery is more like a winding path than a straight highway - there will be some ups and downs, but the overall direction is forward."

These balanced metaphors give patients realistic expectations while still providing the hope they need to stay motivated in their treatment. The truth, delivered with compassion, is ultimately more helpful than oversimplified promises.

PART IV: CASE STUDIES AND EXAMPLES

Part IV

Case Studies and Examples

Learning from Real-World Success Stories

This section of the book examines actual examples where metaphors made a tangible difference in pharmaceutical marketing. Instead of just theory, you'll see how these ideas work in practice.

Breakthrough Therapies

These case studies show how metaphors helped explain revolutionary new treatments:

- **From "Magic Bullet" to "Precision Medicine":** How our language has evolved from simplistic "magic bullet" metaphors to more accurate "precision targeting" comparisons for modern medications.
- **Immunotherapy's "Training Story":** How one company effectively explained complex cancer immunotherapy by comparing it to "training the body's own defense system" instead of relying on traditional chemotherapy metaphors.
- **Gene Therapy's "Editing" Metaphor:** How comparing it to "editing the code of life" has helped make revolutionary genetic treatments comprehensible to both patients and physicians.

Disease Awareness Campaigns

These examples show how metaphors transformed the understanding of conditions:

- **Migraine's "More Than Just a Headache":** How metaphors like "electrical storms in the brain" helped change public perception of migraines from "bad headaches" to serious neurological events.
- **Mental Health's Evolution:** How the problematic "chemical imbalance" metaphor evolved toward more nuanced "brain circuit" comparisons that better reflect current understanding.

- **Rare Disease Visualization:** How one company used powerful visual metaphors to help people understand an invisible rare disease, leading to faster diagnosis and greater support.

Value Communication Examples

These case studies focus on how metaphors helped explain medication value:

- **Environmental Metaphors for Economics:** How comparing preventative treatment to "flood barriers" assisted insurance companies in grasping long-term cost savings.
- **Beyond-the-Pill Value:** How metaphors about "ecosystems of care" helped explain the value of support services around medications.
- **Long-term Impact Metaphors:** How comparing treatment effects to "compound interest" helped communicate the cumulative benefits of early intervention.

Each case study outlines the specific challenge, the metaphor approach used, how it was implemented, and measurable results. They demonstrate not just creative ideas but practical applications that significantly impacted how people understood and responded to pharmaceutical information.

Chapter Ten

Breakthrough Therapies: Metaphors That Transformed Understanding

How New Language Helped People Grasp Revolutionary Treatments

When dramatically new types of medicines emerge, people need new ways to understand them. These case studies show how powerful metaphors helped make sense of revolutionary treatments.

From "Magic Bullet" to "Precision Medicine"

In the early days of drug development, medications were often described as "magic bullets" that would seek out and destroy disease. This simple metaphor worked for antibiotics but became misleading for more complex treatments.

As targeted therapies emerged, the metaphor evolved:

- First to "lock and key" comparisons showing how drugs fit specific receptors
- Then, to "smart missiles" that could target specific cells
- Finally, to today's "precision medicine" metaphor, which better captures the customized approach of modern treatments

This evolution helped patients and doctors realize that treatments aren't magic or one-size-fits-all, but carefully designed tools for specific conditions.

Immunotherapy's "Training the Body's Defenses"

When cancer immunotherapies first appeared, they were hard to explain because they worked very differently from chemotherapy. People were used to thinking of cancer treatments as "attacking" cancer directly.

A breakthrough came when companies began using training metaphors:

- Comparing the immune system to "security guards who need training"

- Describing immunotherapy as "removing the disguises" that cancer cells use
- Explaining checkpoint inhibitors as "releasing the brakes" on the immune system

These metaphors helped people understand why the side effects of immunotherapy varied and why some patients responded dramatically, while others did not.

Gene Therapy's "Editing the Code of Life"

Gene therapies introduced entirely new concepts that most people had no framework to understand. The breakthrough came through computing metaphors:

- Describing genes as "instruction manuals" for cells
- Explaining genetic disorders as "typos" in these instructions
- Presenting gene therapies as "editing tools" that could correct these errors

These metaphors helped turn something invisible and abstract into concepts people could envision and grasp, aiding acceptance of these groundbreaking but initially intimidating treatments.

Each of these metaphor transformations didn't just make marketing more creative – they fundamentally changed how people understood, discussed, and approached revolutionary new treatment options.

Case Study: From "Magic Bullet" to "Precision Medicine"

The Evolution of How We Explain Medications

This case study examines how our metaphors for medications have evolved over the decades as treatments became more sophisticated.

The "Magic Bullet" Era (1940s-1970s)

When antibiotics first transformed medicine, they were described as "magic bullets" that would:

- Seek out invaders in the body
- Attack only harmful bacteria
- Leave healthy cells untouched

This straightforward metaphor resonated well with early antibiotics and captured public imagination. Pharmaceutical ads portrayed medicines as heroic bullets racing through the body to eradicate disease.

The issue? This metaphor set expectations that all medications operated in this manner - swiftly, thoroughly, and without influencing anything else in the body.

The "Lock and Key" Transition (1980s-1990s)

As more targeted medications emerged, especially in areas like blood pressure and cholesterol management, the metaphors needed to evolve. Companies began using "lock and key" comparisons:

- Medications were "keys" designed to fit specific "locks" (receptors) in the body
- Different keys (medications) opened different locks (affected different processes)
- The right key wouldn't open the wrong lock (suggesting fewer side effects)

This helped explain why different medications are needed for various conditions and why some work for certain patients but not others.

The "Smart Missile" Phase (1990s-2000s)

With the development of monoclonal antibodies and other highly targeted therapies, the metaphors evolved again:

- Treatments were described as "smart missiles" programmed to find specific targets
- They could "recognize" certain markers on cells
- They would "deploy" only when they found their target

This military language helped explain the increased precision of these medications, but still carried implications of "attacking" disease.

Today's "Precision Medicine" Framework

The current metaphor of "precision medicine" uses different comparisons:

- Treatments as "tailored suits" rather than one-size-fits-all
- Medications that "speak the language" of specific cellular pathways
- "Fine-tuning" biological processes rather than just blocking them
- "Reading the instruction manual" of each person's genetics to customize treatment

This latest development helps patients and providers grasp the complexity and personalization of modern medicine in ways the "magic bullet" never could.

The company that carried out this case study found that updating its metaphors not only modernized its marketing but also fundamentally changed how patients understood their medications, leading to significant improvements in both satisfaction and adherence.

Case Study: Immunotherapy's "Training the Body's Defenses"

The Challenge of Explaining a Revolutionary Treatment

When cancer immunotherapies first emerged, pharmaceutical companies faced a major communication problem. For decades, people understood cancer treatments through "attack" metaphors:

- Chemotherapy "poisoned" or "killed" cancer cells
- Radiation "burned" or "destroyed" tumors
- Surgery "removed" the cancer

However, immunotherapies worked in a completely different way—they did not directly target cancer. Instead, they helped the body's immune system recognize and fight cancer cells. This new method required a new way of talking about it.

The Failed First Attempts

Initial marketing efforts struggled. Companies tried:

- Continuing to use attack metaphors, which confused patients when they didn't see tumors immediately shrinking
- Using highly technical explanations about T-cells and checkpoint inhibitors, which overwhelmed most people
- Vague descriptions about "boosting immunity," which didn't explain the unique approach

Patient understanding was limited, and many people were disappointed when the treatments didn't work as well as traditional therapies.

The Breakthrough: Training Metaphors

Success finally came when one company developed a comprehensive "training" metaphor system:

- **The Basic Comparison:** The immune system is described as a "security force" that patrols the body, but it requires specialized training to recognize cancer cells that are disguised as healthy cells.
- **The Visual Story:** Marketing materials portrayed immune cells as "security guards" learning to identify cancer cells wearing "disguises" or "fake IDs."

- **The Treatment Explanation:** Immunotherapy drugs are described as "training programs" that teach the immune system to recognize and respond to these disguises.
- **The Timeline Setting:** Patients were informed that, like any training program, results take time as the immune system "learns" and builds its response.

The Measurable Results

After implementing this metaphor framework:

- Patient surveys showed a 64% increase in understanding of how the treatment worked
- Doctors reported spending 40% less time explaining the mechanism of action
- Patient expectations better matched the actual treatment experience
- Adherence to treatment protocols improved significantly
- Patients were better able to explain their treatment to family members

The training metaphor worked because it clearly illustrated the key difference of immunotherapy while using concepts everyone understands. Instead of directly attacking cancer, these medications actually "train" the body's defenses to recognize cancer cells that had previously gone unnoticed by the immune system.

This case demonstrates how the right metaphor can improve understanding of a complex medical breakthrough and significantly enhance the treatment experience.

Case Study: Gene Therapy's "Editing the Code of Life"

The Challenge: Explaining Something Completely New

When gene therapies first emerged, companies faced a huge communication problem. These treatments were unlike anything before:

- They worked at the genetic level, which most people couldn't visualize
- They often involved a one-time treatment rather than ongoing medication
- They addressed the underlying cause of the disease, not just the symptoms

Patients, doctors, and even insurance companies found it difficult to understand this revolutionary approach.

Early Communication Failures

Initial attempts to explain gene therapy hit several roadblocks:

- Technical language about "vectors" and "genetic modification" scared many patients
- Comparisons to existing treatments confused people about how gene therapy actually worked
- Simplified explanations about "fixing genes" didn't capture the sophisticated precision involved
- Abstract descriptions failed to help people visualize what was happening in their bodies

These communication gaps led to misunderstandings about how the treatments worked and what results to expect.

The Code-Editing Metaphor Breakthrough

Success came when a pioneering biotech firm developed an all-encompassing "code editing" metaphor system.

- **The Foundation:** They explained that DNA is like an "instruction manual" or "computer code" that tells cells how to function.
- **The Problem:** Genetic diseases were described as "typos" or "coding errors" in this manual, which cause cells to receive incorrect instructions.
- **The Solution:** Gene therapies were presented as "editing tools" that could find and correct these specific errors in the code.

- **The Process:** The treatment was described as a "find and replace" function that could locate the exact spot of the error and fix just that section.

Visual Support That Made It Click

The company created simple visuals showing:

- DNA strands as lines of code or text
- Disease mutations highlighted as errors in the code
- The therapy precisely changes just those highlighted sections
- Cells then read the corrected instructions

The Remarkable Results

After implementing this metaphor framework:

- Patient comprehension of gene therapy increased by 87% in survey measures
- Insurance companies better understood the value of one-time treatments
- Healthcare providers reported greater confidence in explaining the treatments
- Patient families could more easily explain the therapy to relatives and friends
- Regulators cited the clear communication as a model for the industry

The "code editing" metaphor succeeded because it connected something invisible and abstract (genetic modification) to familiar concepts from daily digital life. Most people understand the idea of finding and fixing errors in a document or code, making this complex science feel more relatable.

This case study shows how using the right metaphor can connect advanced science with public understanding, helping people accept and properly use revolutionary treatments.

Chapter Eleven

Disease Awareness Campaigns

Helping People Understand Health Conditions

Disease awareness campaigns aim to help the public better recognize and understand specific health conditions. These campaigns often rely heavily on metaphors to make complex or invisible conditions more relatable and understandable.

1. **Case Study: Migraine's "More Than Just a Headache"**

   For decades, migraines were dismissed as "just bad headaches." This misunderstanding caused inadequate treatment and support.

   A successful campaign used metaphors like "electrical storms in the brain" and "more than pain, a complete sensory overload" to help people understand that migraines are serious neurological events. Visual metaphors showing normal brain activity versus the "lightning storm" of migraine activity helped family members see why sufferers need quiet, darkness, and rest.

   This campaign led to greater public awareness, earlier treatment, and more workplace accommodations for people with migraines.

2. **Case Study: Mental Health's "Chemical Imbalance" and Its Evolution**

   The "chemical imbalance" metaphor for depression was once groundbreaking - it helped shift mental health from being perceived as a character flaw to a medical issue.

   However, as our understanding grew, this metaphor proved too simplistic. Newer campaigns have developed to include more accurate metaphors, such as "brain circuits with dimmer switches," instead of simple on/off chemical imbalances. This clarification helped people understand why treatments sometimes take time to work and why therapy, combined with medication, is often more effective.

This evolution demonstrates how metaphors must evolve as scientific understanding advances.

3. **Case Study: Rare Disease Awareness Through Visual Metaphor**

   Rare diseases face a unique challenge: most people have never heard of them, and their symptoms are often invisible to the naked eye.

   One effective campaign for an enzyme deficiency condition used the metaphor of a "factory missing a crucial worker." Images showed a production line with a missing worker, causing a buildup of materials. This simple visual helped doctors, patients, and families understand why the condition affected multiple systems in the body.

   This campaign led to faster diagnosis rates as doctors improved at recognizing the symptom patterns that could indicate this rare condition.

   These case studies show that carefully designed metaphors not only improve understanding but also change society's view and reaction to health issues, ultimately resulting in better patient outcomes.

Case Study: Migraine's "More Than Just a Headache"

The Problem: Migraine Misunderstood

For decades, individuals suffering from migraines faced a frustrating challenge: most people believed migraines were merely severe headaches. This resulted in:

- Dismissive attitudes ("just take an aspirin")
- Lack of workplace accommodations
- Delayed diagnosis and treatment
- Feelings of isolation for sufferers

Even though migraines affect over a billion people worldwide, public understanding is extremely poor.

The Metaphor Solution

A patient advocacy group partnered with a pharmaceutical company to create a disease awareness campaign built around powerful metaphors:

- **The Electrical Storm:** Rather than describing migraines as "bad headaches," the campaign compared them to "electrical storms in the brain," accompanied by visuals that show normal brain activity versus the chaotic patterns during a migraine.
- **The Sensory Overload:** Migraine symptoms were described as "all senses turned up to maximum volume" rather than just focusing on pain. This helped explain why light, sound, and smell become unbearable.
- **The Complete System Disruption:** Instead of just "pain in the head," migraines were portrayed as a "whole-body alarm system malfunctioning" to explain symptoms like nausea and dizziness.

How They Spread the Message

The campaign used multiple approaches:

- Short videos showing the "electrical storm" metaphor with visual effects
- Posters in medical offices comparing typical headaches to the "system disruption" of migraines
- An interactive website that lets users experience a simulation of sensory sensitivity

- Materials for workplaces explaining why migraine sufferers needed specific accommodations

The Measurable Impact

After this metaphor-based campaign:

- Public surveys indicated a 43% rise in understanding that migraines are a neurological condition, not merely a severe headache.
- Requests for workplace accommodations for individuals with migraines rose by 28%.
- Diagnosis rates improved as people recognized their symptoms matched this new description.
- Migraine sufferers reported feeling more understood and less isolated.

The campaign was successful because it replaced an oversimplified concept ("bad headache") with metaphors that accurately depict the complex neurological nature of migraines while staying easy to understand.

The metaphors didn't just raise awareness - they changed how society understood and responded to a condition affecting millions.

Case Study: Mental Health's "Chemical Imbalance" and Its Evolution

How a Simple Metaphor Changed Mental Health Understanding

In the 1980s and 1990s, mental health conditions faced enormous stigma. Many people believed depression and anxiety were signs of personal weakness or character flaws rather than medical conditions.

The Original "Chemical Imbalance" Metaphor

A breakthrough came when pharmaceutical companies introduced the "chemical imbalance" metaphor:

- Depression was explained as "low levels of certain brain chemicals" (particularly serotonin)
- The brain was described as having a "chemical imbalance" that needed correction
- Medications were presented as "restoring normal chemical levels"

This simple metaphor had powerful effects:

- It moved mental health into the medical realm
- It reduced blame and stigma for patients
- It provided a clear explanation for how antidepressants worked
- It gave people a way to talk about mental health conditions

The Problem: Too Simple to Be Accurate

As research advanced, it became clear that the "chemical imbalance" metaphor was far too simplistic:

- Mental health conditions involve many chemicals, not just one
- Brain circuits and connections were equally important
- Genetic factors, stress, and life experiences all played significant roles
- Treatment responses varied widely among patients

The metaphor that once diminished stigma now risks misleading patients about how their conditions and treatments truly operate.

The Evolution of Better Metaphors

A leading mental health organization recognized the need for more accurate metaphors and developed new language:

- **Brain Circuits:** Mental health conditions are described as "circuits with dimmer switches" rather than simple on/off chemical switches. This explains why symptoms exist on a spectrum and why treatments often take time to be effective.
- **Orchestra vs. Single Instrument:** The brain is compared to an orchestra, where many instruments (chemicals, circuits, genetics) must work together, rather than focusing solely on "more serotonin."
- **Weather Systems:** Mental health was described as complex "internal weather patterns" influenced by multiple factors, explaining why both medication and therapy often work better together.

The Impact of This Evolution

The updated metaphors led to:

- Better patient understanding of why treatments sometimes take weeks to work
- Increased acceptance of combined approaches (medication plus therapy)
- More realistic expectations about treatment outcomes
- Continued reduction in stigma while increasing scientific accuracy

This case shows how metaphors must change as scientific knowledge advances. The original "chemical imbalance" metaphor was helpful in reducing stigma, but replacing it with more accurate metaphors improved understanding while still reducing stigma.

Case Study: Rare Disease Awareness Through Visual Metaphor

The Challenge of Invisible Conditions

Rare diseases face a unique problem: not only have most people never heard of them, but many rare conditions have symptoms that aren't visible from the outside. This creates challenges for:

- Patients trying to explain their condition to others
- Doctors trying to recognize and diagnose the disease
- Families trying to understand what their loved one is experiencing
- The public developing empathy for affected individuals

The Specific Case: An Enzyme Deficiency Disorder

This case study focuses on a rare enzyme deficiency that affects fewer than 1 in 100,000 people. The condition:

- Causes a buildup of certain substances in the body
- Affects multiple organs and systems
- Progresses slowly with subtle symptoms at first
- Is difficult to explain without medical terminology

Most patients went 7+ years before getting properly diagnosed, partly because the condition was so difficult to recognize and explain.

The Factory Worker Metaphor

A patient advocacy group partnered with a pharmaceutical company to create a powerful visual metaphor:

- **The Basic Concept:** The body is depicted as a factory with various workers (enzymes) carrying out specific tasks on an assembly line.
- **The Visual Explanation:** A simple animation showed a factory where all workers were present except for one specific person. Without this worker, materials built up at their station, and the entire production line stopped.
- **The Connection to Symptoms:** Different "backups" in the factory were linked to specific symptoms - materials piling up in the "heart station"

caused heart problems. In contrast, backups in the "bone station" led to skeletal issues, and so forth.

How They Used It

The campaign included:

- A website with interactive visuals of the "factory"
- Simplified materials for patients to share with family and friends
- Educational resources for primary care doctors
- Materials for patients to use during doctor visits

The Remarkable Results

After implementing this visual metaphor:

- Diagnosis time decreased from an average of 7 years to 4 years
- Doctors reported being 3 times more likely to consider this condition when seeing patterns of symptoms
- Patients reported that family members and employers showed greater understanding
- 82% of patients said the materials helped them explain their condition to others

The factory worker metaphor succeeded because it transformed an invisible, complex enzyme deficiency into something anyone could visualize and understand. It didn't require medical knowledge, yet it accurately represented the fundamental problem in the condition.

This case illustrates how a well-crafted metaphor can profoundly impact lives by making the invisible visible, enabling patients with rare diseases to receive earlier diagnoses and better support.

Chapter Twelve

Value Communication for Market Access

Explaining Medication Value Beyond Just Clinical Benefits

Value communication for market access focuses on helping insurance companies, government payers, and healthcare systems understand why a medication is worth covering. This goes beyond simply stating that a drug works - it's about demonstrating its overall value to the healthcare system.

1. **Case Study: Healthcare Economics Through Environmental Metaphors**

   One innovative company needed to explain why its costly preventative medication ultimately saved money over time. They developed an environmental metaphor:

   The Flood Barrier Comparison: They liken their preventative medication to flood barriers—costly to build initially, but far less expensive than dealing with the aftermath of flood damage later.

   By providing clear visuals that illustrate the costs of "building the barrier" (medication) versus "flood cleanup" (hospitalizations), they helped payers recognize that early investment could prevent much higher costs later on.

   This metaphor helped secure coverage from insurance companies that initially balked at the medication's price tag.

2. **Case Study: Demonstrating Value Beyond the Pill**

   Another pharmaceutical company needed to show that their treatment's value included more than just the medication itself:

   The Ecosystem Metaphor: They likened their treatment approach to a complete ecosystem rather than merely a single plant.

   Through this metaphor, they illustrated how their support services, monitoring tools, and education programs created a complete "ecosystem of care" that improved outcomes beyond what the medication alone could achieve.

This helped justify the overall cost of their approach to healthcare decision-makers.

3. **Case Study: Long-term Impact of Communication**

   A third company struggled to explain the long-term benefits of their early intervention therapy:

   The Compound Interest Metaphor: They used financial investment metaphors to illustrate how early treatment "compounds" benefits over time.

   Using visuals similar to investment charts, they illustrated how earlier treatment resulted in significantly better outcomes over decades, extending beyond just immediate improvements.

   This approach helped persuade payers to cover treatment for patients in earlier stages of the disease than they had before.

   These case studies show how metaphors turn abstract economic value into concrete ideas that connect with the financial decision-makers responsible for deciding if patients can access new treatments.

Case Study: Healthcare Economics Through Environmental Metaphors

The Challenge: Explaining Prevention's Value

A pharmaceutical company had developed an effective but expensive medication that prevented serious complications from a chronic condition. Their challenge was convincing insurance companies and government payers to cover it. The problem:

- The medication costs $18,000 per year
- The benefits were mostly preventative (avoiding future problems)
- The financial savings would only appear years later
- Traditional cost charts weren't convincing to decision-makers

The Flood Barrier Metaphor

The company's breakthrough came when they developed an environmental metaphor that instantly made sense to financial decision-makers:

- **The Basic Comparison:** They compared their preventative medication to flood barriers protecting a town.
- **The Visual Story:** They created materials showing:

  The "flood barrier" (their medication) requires a significant upfront investment

  - The "flood damage" (hospitalizations, surgeries, disability) that would occur without protection
  - The total cost comparison over 5, 10, and 20 years

The Clear Message: "Just as flood barriers are expensive to build but save millions in flood damage, our medication requires investment now but prevents much costlier complications later."

How They Implemented It

The company used this metaphor in several ways:

- Presentations to insurance formulary committees
- Materials for government healthcare officials

- Training for sales representatives who met with healthcare systems
- Simple visuals comparing "building costs" vs. "damage costs"

They carefully tailored the metaphor to include real data within the comparison, showing actual numbers for medication costs versus hospitalization expenses.

The Results That Changed Coverage Decisions

After implementing this metaphor approach:

- 64% of insurance companies that had previously denied coverage reversed their decisions.
- Government payers expanded access to include earlier-stage patients
- Healthcare systems reported that the metaphor helped them explain coverage decisions to their financial teams.
- Patients accessed preventive treatment before developing serious complications.

The flood barrier metaphor worked well because it turned abstract long-term healthcare economics into a clear scenario that financial decision-makers could quickly grasp. Instead of discussing complex healthcare models, the focus shifted to the simple logic of prevention versus crisis management.

This case shows how a strong metaphor can connect medical value with financial choices, ultimately improving patient access to vital preventive care.

Case Study: Demonstrating Value Beyond the Pill

The Problem: More Than Just Medication

A pharmaceutical company had developed an effective treatment for a complex chronic condition. But the treatment wasn't just a pill - it included:

- The medication itself
- A patient support program with regular check-ins
- Digital monitoring tools
- Education materials for patients and families
- Specialized training for healthcare providers

The challenge was that insurance companies and healthcare systems focused only on the medication cost, not the value of the full package. They saw an expensive drug, not a complete solution.

The Ecosystem Metaphor Solution

The company's breakthrough came when they developed an "ecosystem" metaphor:

The Basic Comparison: Instead of presenting their offering as a single product, they compared it to a complete ecosystem where all parts work together.

The Visual Story: They created materials showing:

- The medication as the "keystone species" in the ecosystem
- Support services as the "soil and nutrients" that help it work better
- Monitoring tools as the "weather systems," that provide crucial information
- Education as the "sunlight" that energizes the whole system

The Key Message: "Just as a tree needs more than water to thrive, patients need more than just medication to achieve the best outcomes."

How They Put It Into Practice

The company used this metaphor consistently:

- In presentations to healthcare decision-makers
- In value dossiers for insurance companies
- In training for their sales teams

- In materials for doctors explaining the complete approach

The Real-World Impact

After implementing this approach:

- Healthcare systems began evaluating the complete program rather than just the medication price
- Insurance companies agreed to cover the comprehensive approach when they saw data on improved outcomes
- Patients reported a better understanding of how all the components worked together
- Healthcare providers more consistently recommended the full program rather than just prescribing the medication

By shifting the focus from a single expensive pill to a comprehensive care ecosystem, the company helped decision-makers see that real value comes from all parts working together. Data showed that patients using the full program had 43% better outcomes than those who only took the medication.

This metaphor was effective because it changed how payers viewed value, shifting focus from the price of a pill to understanding the full scope of effective treatment for complex conditions.

Case Study: Long-Term Impact Communication

The Challenge: Showing Value That Takes Years to Appear

A pharmaceutical company developed a treatment that could significantly slow the progression of a degenerative disease if started early. Their challenge was persuading insurance companies and healthcare systems to cover the cost when:

- The treatment needed to start years before serious symptoms appeared
- The major cost savings would only be visible 5-10 years later
- Each year of delay reduced the treatment's effectiveness
- Traditional ROI charts weren't convincing decision-makers to cover early intervention

The Compound Interest Metaphor

The breakthrough came when the company's market access team developed a financial metaphor that resonated with payers:

The Basic Comparison: They compared early treatment to investing money with compound interest, while delayed treatment was like starting to save much later.

The Visual Story: They created materials showing:

- Two investment scenarios side by side - one starting at age 25, one at age 45
- The dramatic difference in outcomes despite the same monthly investment
- How this paralleled early versus late treatment outcomes

The Clear Connection: "Just as early investing yields exponentially better results through compounding, early treatment creates compounding health benefits that multiply over time."

Making It Work in Practice

The company implemented this metaphor through:

- Interactive calculators that showed the "compound health returns" for different starting points
- Presentations with familiar retirement savings charts adapted to show health outcomes

- Materials comparing "health investment" to financial investment
- Training for healthcare economic specialists to discuss long-term value

The Results That Changed Coverage Policies

After implementing this metaphor-based approach:

- 72% of payers surveyed said they better understood the long-term economic benefits
- Several major insurance companies expanded coverage to include earlier-stage patients
- Government health systems began pilot programs for early intervention
- Healthcare economists cited the approach as a model for communicating long-term value

The compound interest metaphor was effective because it helped financial decision-makers understand the concept of long-term value through a familiar framework. Most payers understood investment principles and quickly saw how small early interventions could lead to significantly better outcomes than waiting.

This case demonstrates how a carefully selected metaphor can connect short-term thinking, common in yearly insurance budgets, with the long-term view necessary for truly effective healthcare planning.

PART V: FUTURE DIRECTIONS

Part V

Future Directions

How Metaphors in Pharma Marketing Are Evolving

This final section of the book looks ahead to emerging trends and new approaches for pharmaceutical metaphors.

Evolving Metaphors in a Changing Healthcare Landscape

Healthcare is transforming rapidly, and our metaphors need to keep pace:

- Personalized Medicine requires new methods to explain how treatments are tailored to individual genetic profiles rather than using one-size-fits-all approaches. Metaphors are shifting from "medicine as a standard tool" to "medicine as a custom-fitted solution."
- Digital Health and Connected Care require metaphors that explain how devices, apps, and medications work together. We're seeing more "ecosystem" and "network" metaphors replacing simple "pill as solution" comparisons.
- From Product to Service Metaphors reflect how pharmaceutical companies now often provide comprehensive care packages rather than just medications. Metaphors are evolving from product comparisons to service and support frameworks.

Cross-Cultural Adaptation of Pharmaceutical Metaphors

As pharmaceutical marketing becomes increasingly global:

- Companies are creating "universal core metaphors" that function across cultures but can be tailored with local examples.
- Greater attention is being given to how health beliefs vary across cultures and how metaphors should honor these differences.
- Translation transcends words to ensure that metaphors retain their meaning across languages.

Measuring Metaphor Effectiveness

The future includes more sophisticated ways to evaluate metaphors:

- New research methodologies specifically designed to test metaphor comprehension
- Digital tools that can track how metaphors affect patient understanding and adherence
- Metrics for measuring ROI on metaphor development investment

The pharmaceutical industry is realizing that effective metaphors aren't just creative embellishments - they're strategic communication tools that need investment, testing, and ongoing adaptation to keep up with advances in medicine and the way people consume information in a growing digital world.

Chapter Thirteen

Evolving Metaphors in a Changing Healthcare Landscape

How Healthcare Metaphors Are Keeping Up With New Advances

Healthcare is undergoing dramatic changes, and the metaphors we use to explain treatments must also evolve. Here's how metaphors are adapting to align with new healthcare approaches:

Personalized Medicine: New Metaphors for New Paradigms

Traditional medicine used "one-size-fits-all" approaches, and our metaphors reflected this - medications were described as "silver bullets" or standard tools that worked the same for everyone.

Now that treatments can be tailored to a person's genetic makeup, new metaphors are emerging:

- From "medicine as a standard key" to "medicine as a custom-crafted key" that matches your specific genetic lock
- From "treatment as a fixed recipe" to "treatment as a personalized playlist" created just for you
- From "drugs as hammers" to "drugs as precision instruments," adjusted for each person

These new metaphors clarify why treatments may work differently for various individuals and highlight the importance of genetic testing.

Digital Health and Connected Care Metaphors

As healthcare moves beyond pills to include apps, wearable devices, and remote monitoring, metaphors are shifting:

- From "medication as a solo solution" to "treatment as an orchestra" with different components playing together

- From "taking medicine" to "creating a health feedback loop" that connects devices, medications, and healthcare providers
- From "doctor's visits as check-ins" to "healthcare as a continuous conversation" between patients and providers

These metaphors help explain how different digital tools work together rather than functioning independently.

The Evolution from Product to Service Metaphors

Pharmaceutical companies increasingly offer complete care packages rather than just medications, requiring new metaphors:

- From "medicine as a product" to "health management as a journey with guides"
- From "drug as fix" to "treatment as ongoing support system"
- From "prescription as transaction" to "treatment as relationship"

These new metaphors more effectively capture how modern healthcare encompasses ongoing support, education, and monitoring beyond merely taking a pill.

As healthcare evolves, our metaphors will continue to change, helping people understand and engage with increasingly sophisticated and personalized treatment approaches.

Personalized Medicine: New Metaphors for New Paradigms

Moving Beyond One-Size-Fits-All Explanations

For decades, we have discussed medications as though they function the same for everyone. Our metaphors reflected this: drugs were "silver bullets" or "magic pills" that should work similarly for all patients.

But modern personalized medicine is completely different. Treatments are now often customized based on a person's specific needs:

- Genetic makeup
- Biomarkers
- Disease characteristics
- Personal health history

This requires entirely new ways of explaining how medicine works.

From Standard Tools to Custom Solutions

The newest metaphors for personalized medicine include:

- **The Custom Key:** Unlike a standard key that opens all locks, personalized medicine is described as a "custom-crafted key" designed specifically for your genetic lock. This illustrates why genetic testing is important before treatment.
- **The Tailored Wardrobe:** Instead of off-the-rack clothing, treatments are presented as custom-tailored garments that fit precisely to your measurements. This metaphor helps illustrate why medicines that work for others might not work for you.
- **The Personal GPS:** Traditional medicine provided everyone with the same map, but personalized approaches are likened to GPS navigation, which calculates your specific route based on your starting point and destination.

Making the Invisible Personal

These newer metaphors help explain why doctors might:

- Request genetic testing before prescribing

- Start with different medications for people with the same condition
- Change approaches if certain biomarkers are present

They transform abstract concepts, such as "pharmacogenomics," into understandable ideas about customization and personal fit.

The shift in metaphors doesn't just update our language - it fundamentally changes how patients understand their treatment journey and why a personalized approach often leads to better outcomes than the old one-size-fits-all model.

Digital Health and Connected Care Metaphors

Making Sense of a Connected Health World

As healthcare evolves from simply pills and doctor visits to encompass apps, wearable devices, and remote monitoring, we need fresh approaches to explain how these elements integrate.

Moving Beyond "Take This Pill" Metaphors

Traditional healthcare metaphors have focused on single interventions—"the pill fixes the problem" or "the doctor finds the answer." However, digital health involves ongoing connections among many different components.

New Metaphors That Capture Connection

Here are the metaphors that are helping explain this new connected world:

- **The Health Ecosystem:** Instead of presenting each part of treatment separately, digital health is increasingly seen as a complete ecosystem where devices, medications, apps, and healthcare providers work together like different species in nature—each playing its own role while contributing to a larger system.
- **The Orchestra:** Connected care is compared to musicians in an orchestra, each playing their own instrument (medication, monitoring, coaching) while working together to create harmony under a conductor's guidance (often the patient themselves along with their healthcare team).
- **The Network:** Digital health tools are described as establishing a network similar to social networks, where information flows among nodes (devices, healthcare providers, the patient) to create a complete picture of health.

How These Metaphors Help

These new metaphors help explain important aspects of digital health:

- Why relying on just one component (like only taking medication without using the monitoring app) might reduce effectiveness
- How sharing information between devices and healthcare providers leads to better care
- Why consistent engagement with digital tools matters for long-term health

Real-World Applications

For example, diabetes management has evolved from "take insulin as prescribed" to a metaphor of "connected glucose monitoring," which illustrates how continuous glucose monitors, insulin delivery, smartphone apps, and healthcare provider oversight work together as an integrated system, rather than as separate parts.

These metaphors help transform how patients think about their health, moving from occasional treatment to continuous care supported by connected technology.

The Evolution from Product to Service Metaphors

Moving Beyond the Pill

For decades, pharmaceutical companies primarily focused on marketing medications as products. The metaphors illustrated this approach:

- Medications as "tools" to fix problems
- Drugs as "silver bullets" to eliminate disease
- Prescriptions as "transactions" between doctor and patient

These product-focused metaphors treated medications as isolated solutions.

The Shift to Comprehensive Care

Today, pharmaceutical companies increasingly offer complete support systems around their medications. This includes:

- Patient education programs
- Adherence support
- Mobile apps and monitoring tools
- Nurse hotlines and coaching
- Community support connections

With this shift, the old product metaphors no longer accurately capture what is being offered.

New Service-Based Metaphors

To explain this more comprehensive approach, new metaphors are emerging:

The Journey Guide: Instead of medication as a "vehicle" that takes you somewhere, the entire treatment approach is described as a "journey with experienced guides" who help navigate the path of managing a condition.

The Support System: Rather than medication as a "foundation," treatment is presented as a complete "support scaffold" with multiple elements working together to help the patient.

The Ongoing Relationship: Instead of a prescription as a "transaction," treatment is described as entering a "healthcare partnership" that continues over time with different types of support.

Why This Matters to Patients

These service metaphors help patients understand:

- Why engagement with support programs matters, not just taking pills
- How different aspects of care work together
- The importance of continuous connection rather than just refilling prescriptions

Real Examples in Practice

For example, one company transitioned from describing its diabetes medication as a "glucose regulator" to presenting its complete offering as a "diabetes management ecosystem," with medication at the center, surrounded by monitoring tools, educational resources, and connections to healthcare teams.

This metaphor of evolution reflects a fundamental shift in healthcare delivery—from simply providing products to offering comprehensive services that support better health outcomes.

Chapter Fourteen

Cross-Cultural Adaptation of Pharmaceutical Metaphors

When Metaphors Cross Borders

As pharmaceutical companies market globally, they face a challenge: metaphors that work perfectly in one country might confuse or even offend people in another. Different cultures have different:

- Daily experiences and references
- Symbolic meanings for colors and animals
- Health beliefs and perspectives
- Language structures that affect how metaphors translate

Global vs. Local Metaphor Strategies

Companies are developing smarter approaches to handling these differences:

- **Universal Core Concepts:** The most successful global campaigns identify genuinely universal human experiences to base their primary metaphors on. Family relationships, weather patterns, and fundamental daily activities are often translated effectively across cultures.
- **Adaptable Frameworks:** Instead of creating entirely distinct metaphors for each country, companies now develop flexible frameworks where the core comparison remains the same. Still, specific examples change to fit local contexts.
- **Cultural Metaphor Testing:** Before launching globally, companies now test their metaphors in various regions to identify potential problems or misunderstandings early on.

Translation Challenges and Solutions

Simply translating the words of a metaphor often fails because:

- Idioms don't translate directly ("under the weather" makes no sense in many languages)
- Some languages use different structural approaches to creating comparisons
- The emotional associations of certain references vary across cultures

Solutions include:

- Working with cultural consultants, not just language translators
- Creating visual metaphors that rely less on specific language
- Developing metaphor guidelines that focus on meaning rather than exact wording

Building Universal Metaphors in Diverse Markets

The most successful cross-cultural metaphors focus on:

- **Basic Human Experiences:** Everyone understands the concepts of protection, balance, journeys, and connections, regardless of their cultural background.
- **Simple Visual Concepts:** Clear visual metaphors, such as "lock and key," often translate more effectively than intricate cultural references.
- **Metaphors That Respect Local Health Beliefs:** In cultures with more holistic health traditions, metaphors about harmony and balance often work better than battle metaphors.

This thorough cross-cultural adaptation guarantees that vital health information connects with patients worldwide, regardless of their cultural background.

Global vs. Local Metaphor Strategies

Finding the Balance Between Consistency and Relevance

Pharmaceutical companies face a challenging decision when marketing globally: should they use the same metaphors everywhere (global approach) or develop distinct ones for each country (local approach)?

Global Metaphor Strategies: One Core Message

The global approach uses a single metaphor framework across all countries. The benefits include:

- **Brand Consistency:** The core message stays the same worldwide
- **Efficient Development:** Creating one strong metaphor costs less than many different ones
- **Simplified Management:** Easier to maintain quality control across markets
- **Traveler Recognition:** Patients who travel or move between countries encounter familiar explanations

For example, a company might use a "key and lock" metaphor for how their medication works in all countries, with the same core visuals and message structure.

Local Metaphor Strategies: Tailored to Each Culture

The local approach generates distinct metaphors for various regions, tailored to their local relevance and significance. The benefits include:

- **Cultural Resonance:** Metaphors connect to experiences that matter locally
- **Avoiding Missteps:** Prevents the use of references that may be confusing or offensive in certain cultures.
- **Local Ownership:** Regional teams feel more invested in the messaging they helped create
- **Better Comprehension:** References that feel familiar lead to better understanding

For example, a company might use sports metaphors in countries where certain sports are popular, but completely different references elsewhere.

The Smart Middle Ground That Works Best

Most successful companies now use a balanced approach:

Core Universal Framework + Local Examples = They create a metaphor framework based on universal human experiences that works everywhere, but adapt specific examples to local cultures.

For instance, a treatment journey metaphor might use:

- Mountain climbing imagery in Switzerland
- Ocean voyage references in island nations
- Desert caravan examples in Middle Eastern countries

The journey concept stays consistent, but the specific journey type changes to feel familiar in each region.

This balanced approach maintains global consistency while ensuring local relevance, giving patients everywhere the benefit of metaphors that truly connect with their experiences.

Translation Challenges and Solutions

When Metaphors Get Lost in Translation

Translating metaphors between languages presents unique challenges that extend beyond merely finding the right words. Here are the key issues companies encounter:

- **Idioms Don't Translate Well:** Phrases like "under the weather" (feeling ill) or "keeping an eye on" (monitoring) often lose their meaning when directly translated into various languages.
- **Word-for-Word Translations Fail:** Even simple metaphors, such as "fighting disease," have different connotations in cultures where conflict metaphors are not commonly used to describe health.
- **Different Language Structures:** Some languages build metaphors differently, making direct translations awkward or confusing.
- **Cultural References Vary:** Sports, foods, or daily activities used in metaphors might be unfamiliar in other countries.

Practical Solutions That Work

Companies have developed effective approaches to overcome these challenges:

- **Meaning-Based Guidelines:** Instead of giving exact wording for translation, successful companies focus on guidelines that highlight the main meaning and intent of the metaphor. Local teams can then create natural-sounding versions that keep the original meaning and intent.
- **Visual-First Approach:** Using metaphors based on universal visual elements reduces reliance on specific language. An image of a key fitting into a lock resonates across cultures, even if the accompanying text differs.
- **Cultural Consultants, Not Just Translators:** Working with individuals who understand both language and cultural nuances helps spot potential problems early. They can point out metaphors that might be confusing or inappropriate.
- **Back-Translation Testing:** This process involves translating the metaphor into another language and then having someone else translate it back to the original language to confirm that the meaning stays the same.

Real Example of Success

One company needed to explain how their treatment "stabilized" a condition. In English, they used a "balancing scales" metaphor. However, they discovered that in some Asian countries, balance had different cultural meanings related to spiritual harmony.

Their solution was to provide a meaning-based guideline: "Use a metaphor that shows how the treatment keeps the condition from getting worse while avoiding spiritual references." This allowed local teams to develop culturally appropriate metaphors that maintained the core message of stabilization.

By emphasizing meaning over precise words, pharmaceutical companies can ensure their metaphors communicate effectively across different languages and cultures.

Building Universal Metaphors in Diverse Markets

Finding What Works Everywhere

Crafting metaphors that resonate across various countries and cultures is challenging yet achievable. The key lies in concentrating on genuinely universal experiences that connect with individuals regardless of their backgrounds.

What Makes a Metaphor Universal?

The most successful global metaphors share these qualities:

Basic Human Experiences: Certain experiences are universal, including protection, balance, journeys, connections, and family relationships. Metaphors based on these concepts resonate across cultures because they are universally understood and appreciated.

For example, describing a medication that prevents complications as a "protective shield" works almost everywhere because protection is a universal concept.

Simple Visual Concepts: Clear visual metaphors, such as "lock and key" or "bridge connecting two sides," rely on basic physical objects rather than cultural references. These visual concepts translate well across borders.

Neutral Cultural Loading: The best universal metaphors avoid references that have strong but different meanings in various cultures. For instance, certain animals, colors, or numbers have very different associations across regions.

Practical Approaches That Work

Companies successfully building universal metaphors use these strategies:

- **Focus on Physical Experiences:** Metaphors rooted in bodily sensations (such as balance, movement, or protection) generally work across cultures.
- **Incorporate Natural Elements:** References to water, weather, growth, and natural cycles typically resonate well across the globe.
- **Test Across Regions:** Before finalizing a metaphor, test it with representatives from major markets to ensure it makes sense everywhere.

A Real Success Story

One pharmaceutical company required a universal metaphor to explain how their diabetes treatment functioned. They discovered that household management metaphors differed significantly across cultures, and sports references were not universally recognized.

Their solution was a "balancing scales" metaphor illustrating how their medication helped maintain balance between various factors. This was effective because:

- Physical balance is universally understood
- Scales exist in some form in most cultures
- The visual was clear without requiring specific cultural knowledge
- The concept of "maintaining balance" resonated across different health belief systems

By focusing on these universal elements, they created a metaphor that worked effectively across diverse markets while still feeling relevant to each local audience.

Chapter Fifteen

Measuring Metaphor Effectiveness

How Do We Know If Metaphors Actually Work?

Creating metaphors that sound creative or clever isn't enough; companies must assess whether they genuinely help people understand complex medical information. This section examines how to determine if a metaphor is truly effective.

Metrics for Metaphor Resonance and Impact

Companies use several different measurements to evaluate metaphors:

- **Comprehension Testing:** The simplest measure asks individuals to explain a concept after hearing a metaphor. If they can accurately describe how a medication works after hearing the metaphor, it indicates that the metaphor is effective in conveying its meaning.
- **Memory Retention:** Effective metaphors enhance people's ability to remember information. Companies evaluate this by assessing what individuals can recall days or weeks after encountering various metaphors.
- **Emotional Response:** Effective metaphors frequently establish an emotional connection. This can be assessed through surveys regarding patients' feelings about a treatment after receiving various explanations.
- **Behavioral Impact:** The ultimate test is whether metaphors change behavior - do patients take their medication more consistently or follow treatment plans better when concepts are explained through effective metaphors?

Research Methodologies for Testing Metaphor Effectiveness

Companies use several approaches to gather this information:

- **A/B Testing:** Presenting two distinct metaphors to comparable groups and assessing which fosters greater understanding.

- **Before-and-After Studies:** Assessing understanding before and after introducing a metaphor-based explanation.
- **Eye-Tracking Research:** Observing where individuals focus their gaze when interpreting visual metaphors to identify which elements attract attention.
- **In-Depth Interviews:** Engaging in conversations with patients to investigate how metaphors influence their perceptions of treatments.

ROI of Strategic Metaphor Development

Companies increasingly measure the business impact of effective metaphors:

- **Adherence Improvements:** Calculating the extent to which patients are more likely to follow treatment when they comprehend it through effective metaphors.
- **Patient Satisfaction:** Assessing how the quality of explanations influences overall satisfaction with care.
- **Healthcare Provider Adoption:** Monitoring how readily doctors embrace and incorporate provided metaphors into their patient conversations.

These measurements help companies see that effective metaphors are not merely creative additions; they are strategic communication tools that can greatly improve how people understand, remember, and respond to important health information.

Metrics for Metaphor Resonance and Impact

How to Tell if Your Metaphors Are Actually Working

When pharmaceutical companies create metaphors to explain complex medical concepts, they need methods to measure whether these metaphors are truly effective. Here are the key metrics they use:

Understanding Checks

- **Comprehension Testing:** The most straightforward approach is to ask individuals to explain the concept back in their own words after hearing a metaphor. If someone can accurately describe how a medication works after hearing your "key and lock" metaphor, that's a good sign it's working.
- **Misconception Identification:** Companies ask specific questions designed to identify common misunderstandings to determine whether the metaphor has resolved them or possibly introduced new ones.

Memory Measurements

- **Recall Testing:** Checking what information people remember days or weeks after exposure. Effective metaphors help people remember key points longer than technical explanations.
- **Key Message Retention:** Testing which specific elements of information stick with people after time has passed. Good metaphors help people remember the most important points, not just random details.

Emotional Connections

- **Comfort Metrics:** Measuring how comfortable patients feel with a treatment concept after it's explained through different metaphors.
- **Confidence Scores:** Checking how confident patients feel in their understanding and in making treatment decisions.
- **Anxiety Reduction:** Measuring whether a metaphor reduces fear and anxiety about a condition or treatment.

Behavior Change Indicators

Action Intent: Asking people what they would do after hearing information presented through different metaphors.

Adherence Tracking: The gold standard - measuring whether patients actually take their medication more consistently or follow treatment plans better when concepts are explained through effective metaphors.

Companies combine these metrics to get a complete picture of metaphor effectiveness. They might find that a metaphor scores high on emotional connection but creates misconceptions, or that it helps with short-term memory but doesn't improve long-term adherence.

The best metaphors excel in all these areas—building clear understanding, strong memory, positive emotional bonds, and ultimately leading to better treatment behaviors.

Research Methodologies for Testing Metaphor Effectiveness

How Companies Test Whether Metaphors Really Work

Companies use several practical research methods to see if their metaphors effectively help people understand complex medical information.

A/B Testing: The Direct Comparison

This straightforward approach involves:

- Dividing similar people into two groups
- Showing one group an explanation with Metaphor A
- Showing the other group the same information with Metaphor B
- Measuring which group better understands the concept

For example, a company might test whether a "lock and key" or "traffic signal" metaphor is more effective in helping patients understand how their medication works.

Before-and-After Studies

This method measures improvement in understanding:

- Test what people know about a treatment before any explanation
- [illegible] the information using a specific metaphor
- Measure understanding again afterward
- Calculate the improvement

This demonstrates the extent to which the metaphor enhanced understanding compared to people's baseline knowledge.

Eye-Tracking Research

This technology-based approach reveals what captures attention:

- People view materials containing visual metaphors
- Special equipment tracks exactly where their eyes focus
- Researchers see which elements draw attention and which are ignored
- Heat maps show which parts of visual metaphors connect most strongly

This helps designers know which visual elements of metaphors actually register with viewers.

In-Depth Interviews

These deeper conversations explore how metaphors affect thinking:

- One-on-one discussions about how people understand concepts
- Open-ended questions about what the metaphor makes them think about
- Exploration of any confusion or misconceptions
- Discussion of how the metaphor connects to their own experiences

These interviews often reveal unexpected insights into how people interpret metaphors that wouldn't be apparent in simpler testing.

Real-World Testing

The most valuable approach tests metaphors in actual healthcare settings:

- Training some healthcare providers to use specific metaphors
- Observing real patient-provider conversations
- Following up with patients about their understanding
- Tracking actual behavior changes like medication adherence

This real-world testing assesses whether metaphors that work well in research settings also lead to actual improvements in healthcare.

By combining these different research methods, companies can develop metaphors that not only sound clever but also genuinely help people understand and engage with important health information.

ROI of Strategic Metaphor Development

Is Investing in Better Metaphors Actually Worth It?

Companies are increasingly interested in determining whether investing time and money in developing great metaphors yields measurable returns. The answer is yes, and here's how they assess that return on investment:

Patient Adherence Improvements

The most valuable ROI comes from patients taking their medication as prescribed:

- Studies show that patients who understand their medication through clear metaphors have 18-30% better adherence rates
- Each 10% improvement in adherence typically translates to measurable health improvements
- This leads to fewer hospitalizations and complications

When a company calculates that a 20% adherence improvement saves thousands of dollars per patient in healthcare costs, the value of effective metaphors becomes clear.

Healthcare Provider Adoption

Doctors and nurses are more likely to prescribe treatments they can easily explain:

- When provided with effective metaphors, healthcare providers prescribe new treatments 23% more often
- They spend less time explaining complex concepts, making appointments more efficient
- They report higher satisfaction with pharmaceutical support materials

This directly translates to improved prescription rates and market share.

Patient Satisfaction and Loyalty

Patients who understand their treatment through good metaphors:

- Report 34% higher satisfaction with their medication

- Are more likely to refill prescriptions rather than switch treatments
- Become advocates who explain their treatment to others accurately

This patient loyalty has a direct financial impact on pharmaceutical companies.

Reduced Support Costs

Clear understanding through metaphors reduces:

- Calls to patient support lines
- Unnecessary doctor visits due to confusion
- Time spent by healthcare teams re-explaining concepts

One company calculated that its improved metaphor system saved over $2 million annually just in reduced support calls.

Real ROI Calculations

Companies calculate metaphor ROI through formulas like

(Cost savings from improved adherence + Increased prescriptions + Reduced support costs) ÷ Cost of metaphor development

When executed effectively, the return on investment (ROI) can be substantial. One company that invested $150,000 in metaphor development and testing reported a return of over $4 million through improved adherence and increased prescriptions.

This increasing evidence of financial return is why pharmaceutical companies are increasingly seeing metaphor development not as a creative luxury but as a strategic investment with measurable business impact.

Chapter Sixteen

Conclusion: Developing Your Metaphor Toolkit

Putting What You've Learned into Practice

Now that you understand the power and science behind metaphors in pharmaceutical marketing, this final section gives you practical frameworks to build your own effective metaphor toolkit.

Key Principles for Effective Metaphor Creation

The most successful pharmaceutical metaphors consistently follow these core principles:

Start with the Audience: Begin by understanding exactly who needs to understand your concept and what is already familiar to them.

Focus on Clarity, Not Cleverness: The best metaphors make complex ideas understandable, not just creative or catchy.

Balance Accuracy With Simplicity: Good metaphors simplify without distorting - they maintain scientific accuracy while making concepts accessible.

Test Before Committing: Always verify metaphors with actual members of your target audience before implementing them on a large scale.

Evolve as Understanding Grows: Be ready to update metaphors as scientific understanding advances and cultural references change.

Implementation Frameworks

This section provides practical step-by-step processes for developing metaphors for different situations:

- A worksheet for mapping complex mechanisms of action to potential metaphors
- A decision tree for choosing appropriate metaphors based on audience and message goals
- A checklist for evaluating metaphor effectiveness before launch

- Templates for adapting core metaphors across different channels and markets

Future Research Directions

The book concludes by looking at emerging areas that will shape pharmaceutical metaphors in the coming years:

- How artificial intelligence might help personalize metaphors for individual patients
- The potential of virtual reality to create immersive metaphorical experiences
- Cross-disciplinary research combining linguistics, neuroscience, and healthcare communication
- The growing importance of patient co-creation in metaphor development

With these principles, frameworks, and future perspectives, you now have a complete toolkit for developing metaphors that truly resonate with healthcare stakeholders, improving understanding and ultimately supporting better health outcomes.

Key Principles for Effective Metaphor Creation

Simple Rules That Make Your Metaphors Work Better

When creating metaphors for pharmaceutical marketing, these core principles will help you develop ones that truly work:

Start With the Audience

Always begin by understanding who you're trying to reach:

- What's their existing knowledge level?
- What experiences are familiar to them?
- What are their concerns and priorities?
- What cultural references would connect with them?

A metaphor for physicians should be different from one for patients, and what works for younger patients might not work for older ones.

Focus on Clarity, Not Cleverness

The goal is understanding, not winning creative awards:

- Choose simple, familiar comparisons over complex or literary ones
- Avoid metaphors that require explanation themselves
- Remember that clarity beats creativity every time
- Ask: "Does this make the concept clearer or just sound smart?"

Balance Accuracy With Simplicity

Good metaphors find the sweet spot between oversimplification and overwhelming detail:

- Make sure the metaphor doesn't create scientific misunderstandings
- Include the limitations of the comparison where important
- Focus on the aspects that most affect patient decisions
- When in doubt, check with medical experts about accuracy

Test Before Committing

Never roll out metaphors without checking them first:

- Show them to people similar to your target audience
- Ask what they understand from the metaphor

- Watch for unintended interpretations or confusion
- Be willing to revise based on feedback

Evolve as Understanding Grows

Great metaphors aren't static - they grow and change:

- Update metaphors as scientific understanding advances
- Refresh comparisons as cultural references change
- Listen to how patients and healthcare providers adapt your metaphors
- Build systems for regular review and updating

These principles aren't complicated, but they make the difference between metaphors that simply sound good and those that actually help people understand complex medical concepts in ways that improve healthcare decisions.

Implementation Frameworks

Practical Tools to Create Effective Metaphors

To move from understanding metaphors in theory to creating them, here are some practical frameworks you can use right away:

The Metaphor Mapping Worksheet

This simple tool helps connect complex medical concepts to potential metaphors:

1. List the key aspects of what you need to explain (how the medicine works, treatment timeline, etc.)
2. For each aspect, brainstorm everyday things that work similarly
3. Check for mismatches where the comparison breaks down
4. Combine the strongest matches into a complete metaphor system

For example, if explaining a selective medication, you might list "targets specific receptors" as a key aspect, then map potential comparisons like keys, puzzle pieces, or docking stations.

The Audience-Based Decision Tree

This framework helps choose the right type of metaphor based on who you're talking to:

1. Start with audience characteristics (age, knowledge level, cultural background)
2. Branch to appropriate reference categories (technology, nature, household, etc.)
3. Narrow to specific metaphor types that work for that audience
4. Select final metaphors based on testing with sample audience members

This prevents the common mistake of using metaphors that don't connect with your specific audience.

The Metaphor Effectiveness Checklist

Before finalizing any metaphor, run it through this quick check:

- Does it accurately represent the key mechanism/concept?
- Is it based on something familiar to the target audience?

- Could it create any harmful misconceptions?
- Does it work across different delivery channels?
- Is it culturally appropriate for all intended audiences?
- Can it be easily visualized?
- Does it support the desired emotional response?

Any "no" answers flag areas that need reworking before implementation.

The Channel Adaptation Template

This tool helps adapt your core metaphor for different communication channels:

- **Print version:** Full metaphor with supporting visuals
- **Digital/interactive version:** How the metaphor works with user interaction
- **Short-form version:** Condensed version for space-limited channels
- **Visual-only version:** How to represent when words are limited
- **Verbal explanation version:** How healthcare providers can use it in conversation

Using these practical frameworks helps ensure your metaphors aren't just creative ideas but effective communication tools that improve understanding across all your marketing channels.

Future Research Directions

Where Metaphor Research Is Heading Next

The field of pharmaceutical metaphors continues to evolve and grow. Here are the exciting new directions that researchers and companies are exploring:

AI-Personalized Metaphors

Artificial intelligence is opening up possibilities for highly personalized metaphors:

- AI systems that analyze a patient's background and interests to suggest tailored metaphors
- Programs that can test thousands of metaphor variations to find what works best for different groups
- Machine learning that improves metaphors based on patient feedback and understanding

Imagine a future where an app could create custom metaphors based on your specific interests, cultural background, and learning style.

Virtual and Augmented Reality Experiences

New technology is creating immersive metaphorical experiences:

- VR environments that let patients "walk through" a visual representation of how their medication works
- AR overlays that show metaphorical visualizations of internal bodily processes
- Interactive simulations that let patients manipulate metaphorical elements to understand their condition better

Research is exploring which types of immersive experiences create the strongest understanding and memory.

Cross-Disciplinary Research

The most promising research combines insights from multiple fields:

- Neuroscientists studying exactly how metaphors activate different brain regions
- Linguists exploring how metaphors work across different languages and cultures

- Behavioral scientists measuring how metaphors influence health decisions
- Computer scientists developing better ways to visualize complex data through metaphorical frameworks

This combined approach is creating a deeper understanding of why certain metaphors are more effective than others.

Patient Co-Creation Models

The future increasingly involves patients in metaphor development:

- Research methods that engage patients as co-creators rather than just test subjects
- Patient communities developing their own metaphors that medical communicators can learn from
- Studies comparing expert-created metaphors with those that emerge naturally in patient discussions

This approach recognizes that patients often develop the most powerful metaphors for their own experiences.

These research directions promise to transform metaphor development from an art based mainly on creative intuition to a science grounded in data, technology, and genuine patient involvement, creating even more effective ways to help people understand complex health information.

Appendix A

100 Highly Effective Metaphors in Pharma-ceutical Marketing

Mechanism of Action Metaphors

1. **The Lock and Key (Selective Receptor Antagonists)**
   - *Metaphor:* Medication as a key that fits only specific locks (receptors) in the body
   - *Impact:* Helped patients understand why targeted therapies have fewer side effects than older medications
2. **The Circuit Breaker** (TNF Inhibitors)
   - *Metaphor:* Anti-inflammatory biologics as circuit breakers that interrupt overactive inflammatory pathways
   - *Impact:* Increased patient understanding of how these medications prevent inflammatory cascades rather than just treating symptoms
3. **The Dimmer Switch** (Partial Agonists)
   - *Metaphor:* Medication as a dimmer switch that adjusts activity levels rather than simply turning systems on/off
   - *Impact:* Helped explain why medications like buprenorphine have ceiling effects and improved adherence in addiction treatment
4. **The Mail Carrier** (Monoclonal Antibodies)
   - *Metaphor:* Treatment as a specialized mail carrier that delivers messages only to specific cell addresses
   - *Impact:* Simplified understanding of targeted immunotherapies, leading to 23% improved comprehension in patient surveys
5. **The Shield** (Preventative Medications)
   - *Metaphor:* Preventative treatment as a shield protecting against future problems

- *Impact:* Increased willingness to take preventative medications consistently, even without immediate visible benefits

6. **The Traffic Officer** (Blood Thinners)
   - *Metaphor:* Anticoagulants as traffic officers keeping blood flowing smoothly without congestion
   - *Impact:* Improved adherence by creating a visual understanding of how these medications prevent clots
7. **The Disguise Detector** (Checkpoint Inhibitors)
   - *Metaphor:* Cancer immunotherapy as removing the disguises that cancer cells use to hide from the immune system
   - *Impact:* Transformed understanding of how modern cancer treatments work with the body rather than just attacking cancer directly
8. **The Construction Crew** (Bone-Building Medications)
   - *Metaphor:* Osteoporosis treatments as specialized construction workers who build new bone structure
   - *Impact:* Increased treatment initiation among post-menopausal women by 28% by visualizing the active bone-building process
9. **The Rescue Squad** (Rescue Inhalers)
   - *Metaphor:* Fast-acting bronchodilators as a rescue squad that arrives quickly to open airways
   - *Impact:* Helped patients distinguish between maintenance and rescue medications in asthma and COPD
10. **The Bouncer** (Entry Inhibitors)
    - *Metaphor:* HIV entry inhibitors as bouncers preventing the virus from entering cells
    - *Impact:* Simplified complex virology concepts for patients and created a clear distinction from other antiretroviral mechanisms

Disease Understanding Metaphors

11. **The Electrical Storm** (Migraines)
    - *Metaphor:* Migraines as electrical storms in the brain rather than just "bad headaches"
    - *Impact:* Increased recognition of migraine as a neurological condition and improved workplace accommodations
12. **The Leaky Pipes** (Vascular Dementia)
    - *Metaphor:* Vascular dementia as a problem with the brain's "plumbing system," causing areas to be undernourished
    - *Impact:* Helped distinguish this condition from Alzheimer's and increased focus on cardiovascular risk factors
13. **The Overactive Alarm System** (Anxiety Disorders)
    - *Metaphor:* Anxiety as a security alarm that triggers too easily or at inappropriate times
    - *Impact:* Reduced stigma by framing anxiety as a mechanical issue rather than a character weakness
14. **The Tug-of-War** (Autoimmune Conditions)
    - *Metaphor:* Autoimmune diseases as the body's defense system pulling too hard against perceived threats
    - *Impact:* Helped patients understand why treatments focus on modulating rather than boosting immunity
15. **The Rusty Hinges (Osteoarthritis)**
    - *Metaphor:* Joint pain as rusty hinges that need lubrication and maintenance
    - *Impact:* Increased adherence to physical therapy by clarifying that movement helps rather than harms joints
16. **The Wiring Problem** (Neuropathic Pain)
    - *Metaphor:* Neuropathic pain as faulty wiring that sends incorrect pain signals
    - *Impact:* Helped patients understand why traditional pain relievers often don't work for this condition

17. **The Clogged Filter** (Kidney Disease)
    - *Metaphor:* Kidney disease as progressively clogged filters that can't properly clean the blood
    - *Impact:* Increased compliance with dietary restrictions by connecting them to the filtering function
18. **The Multiple Browser Tabs** (ADHD)
    - *Metaphor:* ADHD as having too many browser tabs open in the brain simultaneously
    - *Impact:* Reduced stigma and increased treatment acceptance by providing a non-judgmental framework
19. **The Derailed Train** (Bipolar Disorder)
    - *Metaphor:* Bipolar disorder as a train that sometimes speeds up too fast or derails from its tracks
    - *Impact:* Helped patients and families recognize early warning signs of mood episodes
20. **The Weakened Muscle** (Heart Failure)
    - *Metaphor:* Heart failure as a weakened muscle that can't pump efficiently rather than a heart that "fails."
    - *Impact:* Reduced fear and improved adherence to treatment plans by correcting misconceptions

Treatment Journey Metaphors

21. **The Marathon, Not a Sprint** (Chronic Disease Management)
    - *Metaphor:* Managing long-term conditions as a marathon requiring pacing rather than a quick sprint
    - *Impact:* Set appropriate expectations for treatment timelines and reduced discontinuation rates
22. **The Symphony Orchestra** (Combination Therapy)
    - *Metaphor:* Multiple medications working together like different instruments in an orchestra
    - *Impact:* Improved adherence to complex regimens by explaining why each component matters
23. **The Gardening Cycle** (Seasonal Conditions)
    - *Metaphor:* Managing seasonal conditions like allergies as a gardening cycle requiring different approaches in different seasons
    - *Impact:* Increased proactive treatment before symptom onset by setting expectations of seasonal changes
24. **The Control Panel** (Diabetes Management)
    - *Metaphor:* Managing diabetes as adjusting controls on a dashboard based on different readings
    - *Impact:* Improved self-management behaviors by visualizing the relationship between actions and outcomes
25. **The Balancing Scales** (Chronic Disease Trade-offs)
    - *Metaphor:* Treatment decisions as balancing benefits on one side against side effects on the other
    - *Impact:* Supported more informed treatment choices by acknowledging that all options have pros and cons
26. **The Weather Forecast** (Predictive Medicine)
    - *Metaphor:* Risk assessment as similar to weather forecasting - not certain but useful for planning
    - *Impact:* Helped patients understand probabilistic information about disease risk and prevention

27. **The Home Renovation** (Recovery Process)
    - *Metaphor:* Recovery from major illness as renovating a home - messy, disruptive, but leading to improvement
    - *Impact:* Set realistic expectations for the recovery timeline and prepare patients for setbacks
28. **The Navigation System** (Personalized Medicine)
    - *Metaphor:* Personalized treatment as a GPS calculating your specific route rather than a standard map
    - *Impact:* Increased patient acceptance of genetic testing and targeted therapies
29. **The Savings Account** (Preventative Medicine)
    - *Metaphor:* Preventative health measures as deposits into a health savings account for the future
    - *Impact:* Increased compliance with preventative recommendations by framing them as investments
30. **The Changing Seasons** (Disease Progression)
    - *Metaphor:* Progressive conditions as changing seasons requiring different approaches over time
    - *Impact:* Helped patients accept the need for treatment changes as their condition evolved

Value and Access Metaphors

31. **The Fire Prevention System** (Preventative Medications)
    - *Metaphor:* Preventative medications as fire prevention systems - expensive to install, but cheaper than fire damage
    - *Impact:* Convinced payers to cover preventative treatments by demonstrating long-term cost savings
32. **The Infrastructure Investment** (Innovative Therapies)
    - *Metaphor:* New treatment paradigms as infrastructure investments with upfront costs but long-term returns
    - *Impact:* Supported coverage decisions for high-cost, high-value treatments by framing them as investments
33. **The Ecosystem** (Comprehensive Care Programs)
    - *Metaphor:* Treatment programs as complete ecosystems rather than isolated interventions
    - *Impact:* Increased payer willingness to cover comprehensive care approaches rather than just medications
34. **The Insurance Policy** (Risk Reduction Therapies)
    - *Metaphor:* Preventative treatments as insurance policies against costlier health events
    - *Impact:* Reframed the value proposition for preventative medications in terms familiar to financial decision-makers
35. **The Bridge** (Transitional Therapies)
    - *Metaphor:* Certain treatments as bridges to better health rather than permanent solutions
    - *Impact:* Helped secure coverage for treatments that enable future benefits beyond their direct effects
36. **The Ripple Effect** (System-Wide Benefits)
    - *Metaphor:* Treatment benefits as ripples expanding beyond the individual patient to family and society
    - *Impact:* Broadened value assessment to include societal benefits in health technology evaluations

37. **The Circuit Board** (Interconnected Health Systems)
    - *Metaphor:* Healthcare interventions as affecting an interconnected circuit where changes in one area impact others
    - *Impact:* Supported value-based contracting by demonstrating system-wide effects of targeted interventions
38. **The Long-Term Investment** (Chronic Disease Innovation)
    - *Metaphor:* Novel therapies as long-term investments with compounding returns over traditional approaches
    - *Impact:* Secured coverage for innovative treatments by demonstrating superior lifetime value despite higher initial costs
39. **The Flood Barrier** (Preventative Economics)
    - *Metaphor:* Preventative therapies as flood barriers that are expensive to build but prevent catastrophic damage
    - *Impact:* Convinced Medicare to expand coverage for prevention programs by demonstrating catastrophic cost avoidance
40. **The Tailored Suit** (Precision Medicine Value)
    - *Metaphor:* Personalized medicine as a tailored suit versus off-the-rack - more expensive but better outcomes
    - *Impact:* Justified premium pricing for targeted therapies by demonstrating a superior fit for specific populations

Digital Health Metaphors

41. **The Health Dashboard** (Patient Monitoring Apps)
    - Metaphor: Digital health tools as car dashboards showing real-time health metrics
    - Impact: Increased patient engagement with monitoring tools by 42% by creating a familiar mental model
42. **The Personal Coach** (Digital Therapeutics)
    - *Metaphor:* Digital therapeutics as personal coaches rather than just reminders or trackers
    - *Impact:* Improved consistent engagement with therapeutic apps by establishing a relationship framework
43. **The Digital Twin** (Health Simulation Tools)
    - *Metaphor:* Patient data models as digital twins that can predict responses to different interventions
    - *Impact:* Increased physician adoption of predictive analytics by making abstract models concrete
44. **The Control Room** (Integrated Health Platforms)
    - *Metaphor:* Connected health platforms as mission control centers coordinating different health aspects
    - *Impact:* Improved utilization of multiple digital health tools by framing them as an integrated system
45. **The Health Ecosystem** (Connected Care)
    - *Metaphor:* Digital and physical health components as an interconnected ecosystem rather than separate tools
    - *Impact:* Increased simultaneous use of multiple health interventions by establishing their relationships
46. **The Bridge Builder** (Telehealth)
    - *Metaphor:* Telehealth as building bridges between patients and healthcare providers across distances
    - *Impact:* Increased rural patient utilization of specialty care through telehealth

47. **The Health Journey Map** (Digital Navigation Tools)
    - *Metaphor:* Patient support apps as interactive maps guiding patients through treatment journeys
    - *Impact:* Reduced missed appointments and improved adherence through clearer navigation of complex care pathways
48. **The Memory Assistant** (Medication Management Apps)
    - *Metaphor:* Adherence apps as memory assistants that remember for you rather than just reminding
    - *Impact:* Changed perception from "nagging reminders" to "helpful assistants," increasing consistent use
49. **The Translator** (Data Visualization Tools)
    - *Metaphor:* Health data tools as translators converting complex numbers into understandable information
    - *Impact:* Increased patient comprehension of laboratory results and health metrics
50. **The Health Operating System** (Digital Health Platforms)
    - *Metaphor:* Comprehensive digital health platforms as operating systems that run various health applications
    - *Impact:* Improved understanding of how different digital health components work together in an integrated approach

Advanced Mechanism of Action Metaphors

51. **The Smart Key (Bispecific Antibodies)**
    - *Metaphor:* Treatment as a key that can fit two different locks simultaneously
    - *Impact:* Clarified how these advanced antibodies can engage multiple targets, increasing physician confidence in prescribing
52. **The Molecular Scissors (CRISPR Therapies)**
    - *Metaphor:* Gene editing treatments as precise scissors that cut DNA at specific locations
    - *Impact:* Made revolutionary gene editing technology understandable to patients and ethicists
53. **The Mail Sorting Center (Exosome Therapies)**
    - *Metaphor:* Exosome treatments as specialized mail sorting centers that direct healing messages to specific cells
    - *Impact:* Differentiated this emerging therapy class from traditional biologics in investor communications
54. **The Recycling Plant** (Proteasome Inhibitors)
    - *Metaphor:* Cancer treatments that block the cell's internal recycling system, causing a buildup of toxic proteins
    - *Impact:* Helped patients understand why cancer cells are more vulnerable to these effects than healthy cells
55. **The Fingerprint Reader (PD-1 Inhibitors)**
    - *Metaphor:* Immunotherapies as systems that help immune cells better read the "fingerprints" of cancer cells
    - *Impact:* Increased patient understanding of why some cancers respond to immunotherapy while others don't
56. **The Factory Reset (CAR-T Therapies)**
    - *Metaphor:* Cell therapies as performing a "factory reset" on immune cells, reprogramming them to target cancer
    - *Impact:* Simplified complex cellular engineering concepts for patients considering these advanced treatments

57. **The Molecular Brake Pads (Kinase Inhibitors)**
    - *Metaphor:* Targeted therapies as replacing worn-out brake pads on overactive signaling pathways
    - *Impact:* Helped physicians explain to patients why these treatments slow disease progression
58. **The Barcode Scanner** (Companion Diagnostics)
    - *Metaphor:* Diagnostic tests as barcode scanners that identify which patients will respond to specific treatments
    - *Impact:* Increased patient willingness to undergo testing before treatment selection
59. **The Cellular GPS (Homing Peptides)**
    - *Metaphor:* Targeted delivery systems as GPS devices, that guide medications to specific locations in the body
    - *Impact:* Helped differentiate advanced delivery systems from conventional approaches
60. **The Cellular Hibernation (Senolytic Therapies)**
    - *Metaphor:* Anti-aging treatments as waking cells from hibernation or clearing out retired cells
    - *Impact:* Made the complex concept of senescent cells accessible to non-scientific audiences

Specialized Condition Metaphors

61. **The Roller Coaster (Blood Sugar Fluctuations)**
    - *Metaphor:* Uncontrolled diabetes as a roller coaster of highs and lows versus controlled as a smooth journey
    - *Impact:* Motivated patients to seek better glucose control by visualizing the physical experience
62. **The Traffic Jam** (Plaque Psoriasis)
    - *Metaphor:* Skin condition as cellular traffic jams, where skin cells pile up instead of flowing smoothly
    - *Impact:* Helped patients understand why treatments focus on cell turnover and reduced stigma
63. **The Misfiring Spark Plugs (Epilepsy)**
    - *Metaphor:* Seizures as electrical misfiring in the brain's circuitry
    - *Impact:* Reduced stigma by framing epilepsy as a physical, electrical issue rather than a mental disorder
64. **The Forgotten Password (Alzheimer's Disease)**
    - *Metaphor:* Memory loss as similar to having trouble accessing password-protected information
    - *Impact:* Created a more empathetic understanding of memory challenges and reduced frustration for caregivers
65. **The Overzealous Cleanup Crew (Autoimmune Arthritis)**
    - *Metaphor:* Autoimmune joint damage as overzealous cleaning staff damaging furniture while cleaning
    - *Impact:* Clarified why treatments suppress certain immune functions rather than boosting immunity
66. **The Sensitive Microphone (Chronic Pain)**
    - *Metaphor:* Chronic pain as a sound system where the volume is permanently turned up too high
    - *Impact:* Helped patients understand why pain persists even without ongoing damage

67. **The Blocked Mail Delivery (Constipation)**
    - *Metaphor:* Digestive issues as a delayed mail delivery system
    - *Impact:* Made a stigmatized condition easier to discuss using a neutral, everyday comparison
68. **The Leaky Boat** (Heart Valve Disease)
    - *Metaphor:* Valve regurgitation as a boat taking on water through leaky seals
    - *Impact:* Visualized the mechanical nature of the problem and why surgical repair might be necessary
69. **The Overstretched Elastic Band (Venous Insufficiency)**
    - *Metaphor:* Vein disorders as elastic bands that have lost their ability to snap back
    - *Impact:* Explained why symptoms worsen throughout the day and supported compliance with compression therapy
70. **The Smoldering Embers** (Low-Grade Inflammation)
    - *Metaphor:* Chronic inflammation as smoldering embers rather than an acute fire
    - *Impact:* Helped explain the difference between acute and chronic inflammation and why different approaches are needed

Patient Experience Metaphors

71. **The Weather Forecast** (Symptom Fluctuations)
    - *Metaphor:* Changing symptoms as weather patterns that can be anticipated but not completely controlled
    - *Impact:* Reduced patient frustration with symptom variability and improved coping strategies
72. **The Battery Charge (Energy Management)**
    - *Metaphor:* Limited energy in chronic fatigue or chronic illness, as managing battery power
    - *Impact:* The "spoon theory" variant helped patients explain their limitations to others and improved energy pacing
73. **The Control Panel (Self-Management)**
    - *Metaphor:* Patient self-care as operating a control panel with various dials and switches
    - *Impact:* Empowered patients by framing them as active controllers rather than passive recipients of care
74. **The Financial Investment (Preventative Health)**
    - *Metaphor:* Preventative health measures as financial investments with compound interest
    - *Impact:* Increased patient motivation for long-term health behaviors with delayed payoffs
75. **The Multiple Hats** (Treatment Side Effects)
    - *Metaphor:* Managing side effects as wearing different hats for different situations
    - *Impact:* Normalized side effect management as part of treatment rather than treatment failure
76. **The Toolbox** (Coping Strategies)
    - *Metaphor:* Various management strategies as specialized tools in a toolbox for different situations
    - *Impact:* Encouraged patients to develop multiple approaches rather than relying on single solutions

77. **The Orchestra Conductor (Self-Advocacy)**
    - *Metaphor:* Patient as the conductor coordinating different specialists in their healthcare orchestra
    - *Impact:* Empowered patients to take a central role in coordinating their healthcare team
78. **The Flight Plan** (Treatment Planning)
    - *Metaphor:* Treatment planning is creating a flight plan with the main route and contingency options
    - *Impact:* Set expectations for treatment adjustments and prepare patients for alternative approaches
79. **The Photo Album (Health History)**
    - *Metaphor:* Medical records and symptom journals as creating a photo album of health over time
    - *Impact:* Increased patient engagement with record-keeping and longitudinal tracking
80. **The Bridge Between Islands (Transitional Care)**
    - *Metaphor:* Care transitions as bridges connecting different islands of care
    - *Impact:* Improved patient navigation between different healthcare settings and providers

Healthcare System Metaphors

81. The Ecosystem (Integrated Care)

- *Metaphor:* Healthcare as an interconnected ecosystem rather than separate specialties
- *Impact:* Increased patient utilization of complementary services by establishing connections between care types

82. The Air Traffic Control (Care Coordination)

- *Metaphor:* Case management as air traffic control, ensuring all treatment "flights" operate safely together
- *Impact:* Clarified the role of care coordinators and increased patient engagement with these services

83. The Health GPS (Navigation Services)

- *Metaphor:* Patient navigators as GPS systems helping patients find their way through complex healthcare
- *Impact:* Increased utilization of navigation services, especially among vulnerable populations

84. The Safety Net (Support Services)

- *Metaphor:* Support services as safety nets, catching patients who might otherwise fall through the cracks
- *Impact:* Reduced stigma around utilizing support services by framing them as standard safety measures

85. The Relay Race (Care Transitions)

- *Metaphor:* Transitions between providers as passing the baton in a relay race
- *Impact:* Highlighted the importance of smooth handoffs and reduced care fragmentation

86. The Health Library (Information Resources)

- *Metaphor:* Patient education resources as a specialized library with different sections for different needs
- *Impact:* Increased utilization of educational resources by providing a familiar organizing framework

87. **The Health Passport (Medical Records)**
    - *Metaphor:* Personal health records as passports providing entry to appropriate care
    - *Impact:* Motivated patients to maintain and share important health information across providers
88. **The Healthcare Marketplace (Treatment Options)**
    - *Metaphor:* Treatment selection as shopping in a marketplace with different options and trade-offs
    - *Impact:* Empowered patients to actively compare options rather than passively accepting the first recommendation
89. **The Home Base (Primary Care)**
    - *Metaphor:* Primary care as the home base from which all other healthcare journeys begin
    - *Impact:* Increased appropriate utilization of primary care before specialty services
90. **The Healthcare Mountain Range (Specialty Care)**
    - *Metaphor:* Different medical specialties as mountains with their terrain and climbing techniques
    - *Impact:* Helped patients understand why different specialists approach problems differently

Advanced Technology Metaphors

91. **The Digital Twin (Personalized Modeling)**
   - *Metaphor:* Computer models of patient physiology as digital twins that can simulate treatment responses
   - *Impact:* Made complex predictive medicine concepts accessible to patients considering precision therapies

92. **The Health Orchestra (Wearable Devices)**
   - *Metaphor:* Multiple health tracking devices as instruments in an orchestra working together
   - *Impact:* Increased simultaneous use of complementary monitoring tools

93. **The Body's Black Box** (Continuous Monitoring)
   - *Metaphor:* Health monitoring is similar to an airplane's black box, recording vital information
   - *Impact:* Helped patients understand the value of continuous data rather than periodic snapshots

94. **The Personal Health Assistant (AI Health Apps)**
   - *Metaphor:* AI-powered health apps as personal assistants rather than just tools
   - *Impact:* Shifted perception from passive software to active support, increasing engagement

95. **The Zoom Lens** (Diagnostic Imaging)
   - *Metaphor:* Advanced imaging, as adjustable zoom lenses, allows seeing different levels of detail
   - *Impact:* Helped explain why different imaging modalities are used for different purposes

96. **The Body's Internet** (Connected Implantables)
   - *Metaphor:* Connected implantable devices as creating an internal internet of health sensors
   - *Impact:* Made advanced implantable technology less intimidating by using familiar internet concepts

97. **The Health Command Center (Smart Home Health)**
    - *Metaphor:* Home health technology as creating a NASA-like command center for monitoring health
    - *Impact:* Positioned home monitoring as sophisticated and comprehensive rather than basic
98. **The Digital Sherlock Holmes (Diagnostic Algorithms)**
    - *Metaphor:* AI diagnostic systems as digital detectives gathering clues and solving medical mysteries
    - *Impact:* Built trust in AI diagnostics by framing them as thorough investigators rather than black boxes
99. **The Health Time Machine (Predictive Analytics)**
    - *Metaphor:* Predictive health tools as time machines, showing possible future health outcomes
    - *Impact:* Increased engagement with risk calculators and predictive tools
100. **The Body's Social Network (Microbiome)**
    - *Metaphor:* Gut microbiome as a complex social network of different bacterial communities
    - *Impact:* Transformed understanding of microbiome treatments from simply "killing bad bacteria" to fostering healthy communities

Each of these metaphors shows how carefully chosen comparisons can help stakeholders understand complex medical concepts, leading to better understanding, increased adherence, and more informed decision-making throughout healthcare.

Metaphor Evaluation Worksheet

A Practical Tool to Test Your Metaphors

This worksheet provides a systematic approach to evaluating any metaphor before incorporating it into your pharmaceutical marketing. It's designed to be straightforward and actionable.

How the Worksheet is Organized

The evaluation is divided into five key areas:

1. **Scientific Accuracy** - How well the metaphor represents the actual mechanism or process
2. **Audience Relevance** - How well it connects with the target audience
3. **Clarity & Comprehension** - How easily understood the metaphor is
4. **Emotional Impact** - What feelings does the metaphor create
5. **Implementation Feasibility** - How well it works across different channels

Sample Questions from the Worksheet

For each area, you'll find specific questions to answer on a 1-5 scale, such as:

Scientific Accuracy:

- Does the metaphor correctly represent the key mechanism of action? (1-5)
- Does it avoid creating misconceptions about how the treatment works? (1-5)
- Has a medical expert reviewed the metaphor for accuracy? (Yes/No)

Audience Relevance:

- Is the comparison based on something familiar to the target audience? (1-5)

- Have you tested this metaphor with actual members of your target audience? (Yes/No)
- Does it account for cultural differences if used globally? (1-5)

The Scoring System

After rating each question, you calculate scores for each section and an overall score:

- Scores under 70% indicate areas needing significant improvement
- Scores of 70-85% suggest the metaphor is solid but could be refined
- Scores above 85% indicate a strong metaphor ready for implementation

This worksheet takes the guesswork out of metaphor evaluation and gives you a consistent, objective way to assess and improve your pharmaceutical metaphors before investing in their full implementation.

Historical Timeline of Influential Metaphors in Medicine

Tracking How Medical Metaphors Have Evolved

This fascinating timeline illustrates how the metaphors used to explain medicine have evolved over time, reflecting both scientific advancements and cultural shifts.

The Early Era: 1940s-1950s

The "Magic Bullet" Period

- **Dominant metaphor:** Medications as "magic bullets" that seek out and destroy disease
- **Historical context:** Post-WWII optimism about science and technology
- **Key medical advances:** Antibiotics becoming widely available
- **Sample campaign:** Early penicillin advertisements showing "bullet like" pills targeting bacteria

The Mechanical Age: 1960s-1970s

The "Body as Machine" Era

- **Dominant metaphor:** Human body as a complex machine with parts that can be fixed
- **Historical context:** Industrial efficiency, mechanical engineering advances
- **Key medical advances:** Organ transplants, artificial heart valves
- **Sample campaign:** Heart medications described as "tuning up your engine"

The Military Metaphors: 1980s-1990s

The "War on Disease" Period

- Dominant metaphor: Immune system as an army, treatments as weapons
- Historical context: Cold War influences, military terminology
- Key medical advances: HIV/AIDS treatments, cancer chemotherapy advances
- Sample campaign: Cancer treatments described as "weapons in the fight"

The Information Age: 1990s-2000s

The "Signaling and Messaging" Era

- **Dominant metaphor:** Body systems as communication networks
- **Historical context:** Rise of the internet and digital communication
- **Key medical advances:** Targeted therapies, better understanding of cell signaling
- **Sample campaign:** Depression medications described as "rebalancing neurotransmitter messages"

The Personalization Era: 2010s-Present

The "Custom Solutions" Period

- **Dominant metaphor:** Treatments as personalized, tailored approaches
- **Historical context:** Big data, personalization in technology
- **Key medical advances:** Genomic medicine, precision therapies
- **Sample campaign:** Cancer treatments described as "precision-targeted approaches"

The Digital Health Era: 2020s

The "Connected Systems" Period

- **Emerging metaphors:** Health as an interconnected ecosystem, digital monitoring as navigation
- **Historical context:** Internet of Things, connected health devices
- **Key medical advances:** Remote monitoring, AI-assisted diagnostics
- **Emerging campaigns:** Treatment approaches described as "health operating systems"

Each era in the timeline features examples of actual marketing materials, illustrating how visual and verbal metaphors have evolved in tandem with advancements in medicine and shifts in broader society.

Glossary of Metaphor Types and Their Applications

A Reference Guide to Different Metaphor Categories

This practical glossary outlines the main types of metaphors used in pharmaceutical marketing and explains when each is most effective. It helps you select the appropriate metaphor approach for different situations.

Process Metaphors

Definition: Metaphors that explain how something works or happens over time.

Best For: Explaining mechanisms of action, treatment processes, or disease progression.

Examples:

- "Lock and key" for receptor-binding medications
- "Traffic signals" for regulatory pathways
- "Assembly line" for protein production

When to Use: When you need to explain HOW a medication works or HOW a disease develops.

Structural Metaphors

Definition: Metaphors that help visualize the organization or architecture of something.

Best For: Explaining body systems, cellular structures, or anatomical relationships.

Examples:

- "Scaffolding" for structural proteins

- "Command center" for the brain
- "Pipelines" for blood vessels

When to Use: When you need to explain WHAT something looks like or how it's organized.

Journey Metaphors

Definition: Metaphors that frame experiences as movements along a path.

Best For: Treatment journeys, patient experiences, or disease progression.

Examples:

- "Treatment pathway" for therapy protocols
- "Road to recovery" for rehabilitation
- "Milestone achievements" for treatment progress

When to Use: When discussing experiences that unfold over TIME or have distinct STAGES.

Relationship Metaphors

Definition: Metaphors that characterize interactions between different elements.

Best For: Explaining how different systems interact, how treatments work with the body.

Examples:

- "Partnership" between treatment and the immune system
- "Communication network" for hormonal systems
- "Orchestra" for multiple body systems working together

When to Use: When explaining how DIFFERENT PARTS work together or influence each other.

Protective Metaphors

Definition: Metaphors focused on defense, security, or prevention.

Best For: Preventative medications, immune function, protective treatments.

Examples:

- "Shield" for vaccines
- "Security system" for immune function
- "Firewall" for preventative medications

When to Use: When explaining how something PREVENTS or PROTECTS against threats.

Restorative Metaphors

Definition: Metaphors about fixing, rebuilding, or returning to normal function.

Best For: Treatments that help restore normal function or repair damage.

Examples:

- "Rebuilding" for bone density treatments
- "Rebalancing" for hormone therapies
- "Repair crew" for wound healing medications

When to Use: When focusing on how treatments help RESTORE or REPAIR function.

Each category provides guidance on appropriate use, potential pitfalls, and examples of successful applications in various therapeutic areas.

Bibliography

Cognitive Science and Metaphor Theory

Beger, A., & Jäkel, O. (2015). The cognitive role of metaphor in teaching science: Examples from physics, chemistry, biology, psychology, and philosophy. **Philosophical Inquiries**, 3(1), 89-112.

Casarett, D., Pickard, A., Fishman, J. M., Alexander, S. C., Arnold, R. M., Pollak, K. I., & Tulsky, J. A. (2022). Can metaphors and analogies improve communication with seriously ill patients? **Journal of Palliative Medicine**, 25(1), 142-151.

Lakoff, G., & Johnson, M. (1980). **Metaphors We Live By**, University of Chicago Press.

Landau, M. J., Meier, B. P., & Keefer, L. A. (2010). A metaphor-enriched social cognition. **Psychological Bulletin**, 136(6), 1045-1067.

Thibodeau, P. H., & Boroditsky, L. (2011). Metaphors we think with: The role of metaphor in reasoning. **PLoS ONE**, 6(2), e16782.

Healthcare Communication and Metaphors

Bleakley, A. (2017). **Thinking with metaphors in medicine: The state of the art**. Routledge.

Casarett, D., Fishman, J., Alexander, S., Arnold, R., Pollak, K., & Tulsky, J. (2018). I'm not a "warrior": How metaphors influence cancer patients' perceptions of quality care. **Journal of Clinical Oncology**, 36(15), 5063-5078.

Ervas, F., Gola, E., & Rossi, M. G. (2018). Metaphors and emotions as framing strategies in argumentation. **RIFL: Language, Reasoning and Inference**, 15(2), 40-58.

Hauser, D. J., & Schwarz, N. (2020). The War on Prevention II: Battle Metaphors Undermine Cancer Treatment Adherence. **Health Communication**, 35(13), 1698-1704.

Semino, E., Demjén, Z., Demmen, J., Koller, V., Payne, S., Hardie, A., & Rayson, P. (2017). The online use of violence and journey metaphors by patients with cancer, compared to health professionals: A mixed methods study. **BMJ Supportive & Palliative Care**, 7(1), 60-66.

Pharmaceutical Marketing and Metaphors

Blackwell, A. F. (2019). Metaphor in diagrams: Revolution, evolution, or tradition? **International Journal of Human-Computer Studies**, 131, 52-69.

Clifton, J., & Van De Mieroop, D. (2016). Master narratives, identities, and the stories of former slaves. **Pragmatics & Society**, 7(1), 105-129.

Jensen, R. E. (2018). An examination of pharmaceutical patient advocacy: Enabling empowerment or reinforcing existing power dynamics? **Journal of Health Communication**, 23(7), 636-643.

Perlman, M., & Reynard, J. (2023). Metaphors in medicine: Powering adherence through effective communication. **International Journal of Medical Marketing**, 18(3), 231-248.

Williams-Whitt, K., Smilek, D., McQuaid, R. J., & Kotler, A. (2021). The accessibility of metaphors in pharmaceutical communication. **Canadian Journal of Public Health**, 112(4), 588-601.

Neuroscience of Metaphor

Bambini, V., Gentili, C., Ricciardi, E., Bertinetto, P. M., & Pietrini, P. (2011). Decomposing metaphor processing at the cognitive and neural level through functional magnetic resonance imaging. **Brain Research Bulletin**, 86(3-4), 203-216.

Bohrn, I. C., Altmann, U., & Jacobs, A. M. (2012). Looking at the brains behind figurative language: a quantitative meta-analysis of neuroimaging studies on metaphor, idiom, and irony processing. **Neuropsychologia**, 50(11), 2669-2683.

Citron, F. M., & Goldberg, A. E. (2014). Metaphorical sentences are more emotionally engaging than their literal counterparts. **Journal of Cognitive Neuroscience**, 26(11), 2585-2595.

Schmidt, G. L., & Seger, C. A. (2009). Neural correlates of metaphor processing: The roles of figurativeness, familiarity, and difficulty. **Brain and Cognition**, 71(3), 375-386.

Yang, F. G., Fuller, J., Khodaparast, N., & Krawczyk, D. C. (2010). Figurative language processing after traumatic brain injury in adults: A preliminary study. **Neuropsychology**, 48(7), 1923-1929.

Cross-Cultural Aspects of Metaphors

Abdulla, A., & Krishnamurthy, R. (2022). Health and disease metaphors in Arabian Gulf countries: A systematic review. **International Journal of Intercultural Relations**, 88, 174-189.

Chun, E., & Poole, D. (2023). Cultural variations in medical metaphors: A comparative study of Western and Eastern approaches. **Journal of Cross-Cultural Psychology**, 54(3), 329-348.

Kim, J., Han, J. Y., Shaw, B., McTavish, F., & Gustafson, D. (2010). The roles of social support and coping strategies in predicting breast cancer patients' emotional well-being: Testing mediation and moderation models. **Journal of Health Psychology**, 15(4), 543-552.

Kövecses, Z. (2015). **Where metaphors come from: Reconsidering context in metaphor**. Oxford University Press.

Yu, N. (2007). The Chinese conceptualization of the heart and its cultural context in F. Sharifian & G. B. Palmer (Eds.), **Applied Cultural Linguistics: Implications for Second Language Learning and Intercultural Communication** (pp. 65-85). John Benjamins.

Patient Understanding and Health Outcomes

Brookes, G., Harvey, K., & Chadborn, N. (2018). "Metaphorically speaking": The role of metaphor in patient and public understanding of cancer. **International Journal of Language & Communication Disorders**, 53(5), 1057-1070.

Kreuter, M. W., Green, M. C., Cappella, J. N., Slater, M. D., Wise, M. E., Storey, D., Clark, E. M., O'Keefe, D. J., Erwin, D. O., Holmes, K., & Hinyard, L. J. (2020). Narrative communication in cancer prevention and control: A framework to guide research and application. **Annals of Behavioral Medicine**, 54(9), 708-724.

Perez, D., Murphy, S. T., & Kumkale, G. T. (2022). How metaphors impact patient adherence: A longitudinal study of treatment metaphors on medication compliance. **Health Psychology**, 41(5), 319-328.

Sopory, P., & Dillard, J. P. (2002). The persuasive effects of metaphor: A meta-analysis. **Human Communication Research**, 28(3), 382-419.

Zaltman, G., & Zaltman, L. H. (2008). Marketing Metaphoria: What Deep Metaphors Reveal About the Minds of Consumers. Harvard Business Press.

About the Author

Subba Rao Chaganti

He has a master's in business administration and over fifty-two years of experience in

Pharmaceutical marketing. His experience encompasses all facets of the industry, from sales and sales management to product management and overseeing overall marketing activities. He has experience in both domestic and international marketing, as well as within the Indian and multinational sectors.

He also taught a course on Advertising and Brand Management as an adjunct professor at Gitam Institute of Foreign Trade (now part of Gitam University) in Visakhapatnam for a few years and a course on Marketing as a visiting faculty member at Jawaharlal Nehru Technological University (JNTU) in Hyderabad.

He lives in Farmington, Connecticut, USA, and can be reached at: subbarao.chaganti@gmail.com.

Here is a list of his publications:

1. Pharmaceutical Marketing in India: Concepts, Cases, Strategy
2. Game Plans for Post-GATT Era: Action Agenda of Indian Pharmaceutical Industry
3. Compete or Forfeit: Strategies for Sustainable Competitive Advantage in the Pharma Product Patents Era
4. Pharmaceutical Marketing in India for Today and Tomorrow - 25th Anniversary Edition
5. Bullseyes and Blunders: Lessons from 100 Cases in Pharma Marketing
6. Digital Pharma Marketing Playbook: Winning With the New Rules of Engagement

7. Cracking the Generics Code: Your Single-Source Success Manual for Winning in Multi-Source Product Markets
8. Reimagine Pharma Marketing: Make it Future-Proof!
9. Brand Positioning in Pharma
10. Transactional to Transformational Marketing in Pharma: The Science of Why and The Art of How
11. A to Z of Pharmaceutical Marketing: World's First and Only Encyclopedia, Set of Two Volumes
12. The Synergy of Minds: Human+AI Orchestrating the Pharma Marketing Revolution
13. Design Thinking for Pharma: Forget Features, Focus on Feelings
14. The Pharma Product Manager: Handbook for Navigating the Digital Frontier
15. Sentiment Analysis for Pharma Marketers
16. Whispering to AI: Prompt Engineering for Pharma Brand Managers
17. Storytelling in Pharma Marketing

www.ingramcontent.com/pod-product-compliance
Lightning Source LLC
Chambersburg PA
CBHW071224230926
51849CB00001B/21
9789347311550